Hands-On IoT Solutions with Blockchain

Discover how converging IoT and blockchain can help you build effective solutions

Maximiliano Santos
Enio Moura

BIRMINGHAM - MUMBAI

Hands-On IoT Solutions with Blockchain

Commissioning Editor: Gebin George
Acquisition Editor: Rohit Rajkumar
Content Development Editor: Deepti Thore
Technical Editor: Rudolph Almeida
Copy Editor: Safis Editing
Project Coordinator: Jagdish Prabhu
Proofreader: Safis Editing
Indexer: Mariammal Chettiyar
Graphics: Jisha Chirayil
Production Coordinator: Aparna Bhagat

First published: January 2019

Production reference: 1030119

Published by Packt Publishing Ltd.
Livery Place
35 Livery Street
Birmingham
B3 2PB, UK.

ISBN 978-1-78913-224-3

www.packtpub.com

`mapt.io`

Mapt is an online digital library that gives you full access to over 5,000 books and videos, as well as industry leading tools to help you plan your personal development and advance your career. For more information, please visit our website.

Why subscribe?

- Spend less time learning and more time coding with practical eBooks and Videos from over 4,000 industry professionals

- Improve your learning with Skill Plans built especially for you

- Get a free eBook or video every month

- Mapt is fully searchable

- Copy and paste, print, and bookmark content

Packt.com

Did you know that Packt offers eBook versions of every book published, with PDF and ePub files available? You can upgrade to the eBook version at `www.packt.com` and as a print book customer, you are entitled to a discount on the eBook copy. Get in touch with us at `customercare@packtpub.com` for more details.

At `www.packt.com`, you can also read a collection of free technical articles, sign up for a range of free newsletters, and receive exclusive discounts and offers on Packt books and eBooks.

Contributors

About the authors

Maximiliano Santos works as an architect for IBM Cloud Garage Sao Paulo. He has developed complex software architectures for the banking, real estate, insurance, chemical, and consumer goods industries. He currently works as a Cloud Garage architect. Max has designed solutions using IBM Watson's cognitive services, an **Internet of Things** (**IoT**) platform, as well as machine learning and mobile applications.

Enio Moura is an enterprise architect and works as a delivery leader at IBM Cloud Garage Sao Paulo. He has 25 years' operational and consulting experience in IT services with a lot of experience in integration systems, cloud computing, architecture design, and blockchain and infrastructure solutions, and also has in-depth knowledge of cloud applications and mobile solutions.

About the reviewers

Fabio Cossini is a digital solutions architect at Avanade Inc., working with clients on their application modernization journeys. He is also a technologist and enterprise architect for general cross-industry and cross-technology solutions focused on digital transformation. Since 2012, he has dedicated his career and academic research to IoT, the cloud, analytics, cognitive computing, and blockchain, supporting companies to redefine their business models.

> *I would like to thank Ênio J. Moura and Maximiliano "Max" Santos for the opportunity to collaborate on this book. Their work will be of great help to those interested in learning IoT and blockchain, and how these technologies will shape the future of business.*

Sanket Thodge is the founder of Pi R Square Digital Solutions Pvt Ltd and is a corporate trainer by profession, based in Pune, India. Sanket is the author of the book *Cloud Analytics with Google Cloud Platform*, and is writing another, *Blockchain with Artificial Intelligence*. With expertise in big data, Sanket has explored the cloud, IoT, machine learning, and blockchain. He has applied for a couple of patents in IoT and has worked with numerous start-ups and MNCs, providing consultancy and corporate training.

Xun (Brian) Wu has over 17 years' extensive hands-on experience of design and development in blockchain, big data, the cloud, UI, and system infrastructure. A coauthor of *Blockchain By Example, Hyperledger Cookbook, Blockchain Quick Start Guide*, and *Seven NoSQL Databases in a Week*, he has also technically reviewed over 50 technical books for Packt Publishing. He serves as a board advisor for several blockchain start-ups and owns several patents on blockchain. He holds a computer science master's degree from NJIT and lives in New Jersey with his two beautiful daughters, Bridget and Charlotte.

> *I would like to thank my parents, wife, and kids for their patience and support throughout this endeavor.*

Packt is searching for authors like you

If you're interested in becoming an author for Packt, please visit `authors.packtpub.com` and apply today. We have worked with thousands of developers and tech professionals, just like you, to help them share their insight with the global tech community. You can make a general application, apply for a specific hot topic that we are recruiting an author for, or submit your own idea.

Table of Contents

Preface

Blockchain and the **Internet of Things (IoT)** have proved to be the most in-demand technologies right now, and are just at the beginning of their adoption curve. The consolidation of blockchain and the IoT is on the priority list of several big companies and a few have already started using its implementations, solutions, and initiatives in several projects.

This book will help you develop a blockchain and IoT solution using best practices.

Who this book is for

This book is for anyone who is responsible for the security mechanisms of an IoT infrastructure, and IT professionals who wish to develop solutions using blockchain and IoT on the IBM Cloud platform. A basic understanding of IoT is required.

What this book covers

Chapter 1, *Understanding IoT and Developing Devices on the IBM Watson IoT Platform*, helps you understand how IoT can be a game changer, what industries can do with this technology, how to get started in the IoT world, and what features the IBM IoT Platform provides and how you can leverage those features when creating an IoT solution.

Chapter 2, *Creating Your First IoT Solution*, helps you create your first end-to-end IoT solution using the platform and a Raspberry Pi to exercise your skills. You will create an automated garden-watering system that uses the platform to keep plants adequately watered.

Chapter 3, *Explaining Blockchain Technology and Working with Hyperledger*, introduces you to blockchain and helps you to understand how it works with a ledger to record the history of transactions that provide a permissioned network with known identities.

Chapter 4, *Creating Your Own Blockchain Network*, helps you create your own blockchain network using Hyperledger Composer, and explores how to create an asset, transaction functions, access control, and query definition.

Chapter 5, *Addressing Food Safety - Building around the Blockchain*, helps you design and implement a solution to address a logistics problem. You will gain an understanding of how an IoT and blockchain solution can ensure that a food chain that starts at a farm and ends on a person's plate can be securely tracked throughout its journey using those technologies, and in order to gain the compliance from many countries that will apply to this practice in a few years.

Chapter 6, *Designing the Solution Architecture*, helps you design the solution architecture from the food safety transportation business problem and define the requirements for a technical solution using blockchain to support the distributed ledger network and IoT devices, and the platform, to support the tracking process.

Chapter 7, *Creating Your Blockchain and IoT Solution*, shows you how to create a blockchain and IoT-integrated solution to address food safety transportation problems. You will gain hands-on experience using blockchain and IoT platforms by coding and testing the components designed in the previous chapter.

Chapter 8, *The IoT, Blockchain, and Industry 4.0*, helps you understand what the industry trends are and what new business models can be created or derived from IoT and blockchain solutions, as well as the market and technical trends regarding these technologies.

Chapter 9, *Best Practices for Developing Blockchain and IoT Solutions*, helps you understand previous project experiences and scenarios, and looks at the best practices and lessons learned for designing and developing blockchain and IoT solutions.

To get the most out of this book

We expect that you have familiarity with a programming language and some experience developing any solution for any embedded platform available (such as Raspberry Pi, Arduino, ESP8266, or Intel Edison). We will mostly be using Node.js and the Hyperledger Composer modeling language. Beginner-level JavaScript skills are welcome.

Download the example code files

You can download the example code files for this book from your account at www.packt.com. If you purchased this book elsewhere, you can visit www.packt.com/support and register to have the files emailed directly to you.

You can download the code files by following these steps:

1. Log in or register at `www.packt.com`.
2. Select the **SUPPORT** tab.
3. Click on **Code Downloads & Errata**.
4. Enter the name of the book in the **Search** box and follow the onscreen instructions.

Once the file is downloaded, please make sure that you unzip or extract the folder using the latest version of:

- WinRAR/7-Zip for Windows
- Zipeg/iZip/UnRarX for Mac
- 7-Zip/PeaZip for Linux

The code bundle for the book is also hosted on GitHub at `https://github.com/PacktPublishing/Hands-On-IoT-Solutions-with-Blockchain`. In case there's an update to the code, it will be updated on the existing GitHub repository.

We also have other code bundles from our rich catalog of books and videos available at `https://github.com/PacktPublishing/`. Check them out!

Download the color images

We also provide a PDF file that has color images of the screenshots/diagrams used in this book. You can download it here: `https://www.packtpub.com/sites/default/files/downloads/9781789132243_ColorImages.pdf`.

Conventions used

There are a number of text conventions used throughout this book.

`CodeInText`: Indicates code words in text, database table names, folder names, filenames, file extensions, pathnames, dummy URLs, user input, and Twitter handles. Here is an example: "Next, open the IDE of your preference, create a new Node.js project, and install the `ibmiotf` dependency package."

A block of code is set as follows:

```
{
  "org": "<your iot org id>",
  "id": "<any application name>",
  "auth-key": "<application authentication key>",
  "auth-token": "<application authentication token>"
}
```

When we wish to draw your attention to a particular part of a code block, the relevant lines or items are set in bold:

```
"successRedirect": "<redirection URL. will be overwritten by the property
'json: true'>",
"failureRedirect": "/?success=false",
"session": true,
```

Any command-line input or output is written as follows:

```
$ npm start
> sample-device@1.0.0 start /sample-device
```

Bold: Indicates a new term, an important word, or words that you see onscreen. For example, words in menus or dialog boxes appear in the text like this. Here is an example: "From the IoT Platform service created in the setup step, select **Devices** in the menu and then select **Add Device**."

Warnings or important notes appear like this.

Tips and tricks appear like this.

Get in touch

Feedback from our readers is always welcome.

General feedback: If you have questions about any aspect of this book, mention the book title in the subject of your message and email us at customercare@packtpub.com.

Errata: Although we have taken every care to ensure the accuracy of our content, mistakes do happen. If you have found a mistake in this book, we would be grateful if you would report this to us. Please visit www.packt.com/submit-errata, selecting your book, clicking on the Errata Submission Form link, and entering the details.

Piracy: If you come across any illegal copies of our works in any form on the Internet, we would be grateful if you would provide us with the location address or website name. Please contact us at copyright@packt.com with a link to the material.

If you are interested in becoming an author: If there is a topic that you have expertise in and you are interested in either writing or contributing to a book, please visit authors.packtpub.com.

Reviews

Please leave a review. Once you have read and used this book, why not leave a review on the site that you purchased it from? Potential readers can then see and use your unbiased opinion to make purchase decisions, we at Packt can understand what you think about our products, and our authors can see your feedback on their book. Thank you!

For more information about Packt, please visit packt.com.

1
Understanding IoT and Developing Devices on the IBM Watson IoT Platform

In today's world, computers are able to process an unimaginable amount of data, and anyone can create and sell their own devices. Because of this, **Internet of Things (IoT)** has become a hot topic in the current business environment, and people are more connected than ever.

In this chapter, you will see how IoT can be a game changer and discover what industries can do with this technology. We will look at how to get started in the IoT world, understand the features the IBM IoT Platform provides, and learn how to leverage these features when creating our own IoT solution.

The following topics will be covered in this chapter:

- IoT as a business and technology
- Industries that are implementing IoT solutions
- Technical elements that are part of an IoT solution
- Features and capabilities available in the IBM Watson IoT Platform
- Creating a simple gateway, application, and device that are integrated into the IBM Watson IoT Platform

What is IoT?

There are many definitions of what IoT is, but the most common articles found on the web agree that it is a set of computerized things interconnected through the internet. Things can be understood as people, objects, computers, phones, buildings, animals, and anything that can be connected to the internet.

The term has been in use ever since embedded systems have been able to connect to the internet and have become participants in the network. From computers to mobile phones, smart watches to thermostats and refrigerators, entire production lines can now be connected to the internet.

This evolution has also been enriched by the DIY community. Around the world, you will find prototyping systems, such as Arduinos, Raspberry Pis, and other **systems-on-a-chip** (**SOC**) available at lower prices; user-friendly programming languages; and even graphical programming.

So, how could a connected refrigerator, for example, benefit you? Well, this type of technology would allow the manufacturer to monitor your behavior and see that you are not at home from 9 A.M. to 6 P.M. each day because the refrigerator door wasn't opened during that time frame for one month. What if the refrigerator could be reprogrammed to reduce usage during that period because no one is going to open the door? What if the same manufacturer looks at the data collected from all the owners of that refrigerator? Getting an insight into what the different groups of owners are and how they interact with the refrigerator daily could make it possible to create a new model based on that information. This solution would be more ecological, customizable, and cheaper. It would also make it possible to update the refrigerator software to make it smarter, without the need for buying a new one.

Apple has released frameworks for the IoT such as **HomeKit** and **HealthKit**. These have different goals, but are still things that are connected to the internet.

People can connect objects such as door/window sensors, cameras, thermostats, light bulbs, and locks to the internet and then use the Home app on their iPhones to control them from anywhere in the world. This makes it possible to obtain automatic changes to thermostats when you are on your way home, or to be notified of things such as an open door when you're outside. It could even notify you of your daily weight, using a connected weight scale. Google, Amazon, and other companies have also introduced similar solutions to these use cases.

The IBM Watson IoT Platform does not intend to deliver a product. Instead, it focuses on delivering a secure, scalable, and reliable platform to act as a connection hub between devices and applications.

Common business use cases of IoT

The refrigerator was a simple and powerful example of using IoT at home, but it's not the only example of how this could be used. In this chapter, we will discuss a few different cases, industries, and people that could benefit from having connected devices.

Connected car

Let's take the example of an autonomous car. With this, automakers can monitor general driver behavior and improve various aspects of the driving experience, as well as security. They can also detect failed components sooner, leading to earlier recalls and thereby improving customer satisfaction while reducing the production costs of problematic components. From the perspective of an automobile owner, this could be beneficial as they could monitor the wear and tear of the car parts and spend less money on maintenance costs.

Connected persons

If you are a sports practitioner, you have probably already used a smartwatch to monitor your fitness. If all of that information was properly stored and analyzed, then medical studies could obtain more data that could predict diseases and maybe even improve overall quality of life.

Furthermore, connecting health devices (such as scales, heart monitors, and blood meters) and sharing data using blockchain could create a unified medical report for each person. Doctors could improve diagnostics and medical decisions as a result. This would also enable disease profiling and prediction.

IoT played a major role in the 2016 Olympics held in Rio de Janeiro. Many connected items were used to gather information and process which factors had an effect on athletes' bodies during matches. This was also helpful for creating new equipment, such as bikes, and new regeneration strategies for intense competition.

These simple examples of how IoT will change our entire way of life provide us with more than one reason as to why we should care about it so much.

Technical elements in IoT

Internet of Things does not rely only on devices and applications. It requires a set of capabilities that, when used in an IoT solution, deliver more value to people and companies. In this section, we will discuss some of these capabilities, such as devices, hardware, and software, that are essential for designing and implementing an effective IoT solution.

Devices

Devices are located at the edge of the IoT solution. In fact, these devices are what we call *Things* in the context of IoT. They are usually capable of sending and receiving data events.

As an example, a device with an embedded soil moisture probe can detect that the monitored soil has 43% moisture. It can then report this informative event to the platform it's connected to. The platform can then send an action event to the device, triggering a water valve to open and restore the soil moisture. This interaction depends on other aspects related to the device, which will be covered in upcoming sections. For now, let's focus on the device.

In order to handle these types of interactions, you may think of a device as a computing unit that has analog or digital (or both) processing capabilities. This means that it is able to read and write analog and digital signals to their probes and actuators.

An analog signal is a signal that can vary in a range of values. Let's take an Arduino Uno board, for example. Arduino Uno has a 10-bit resolution **analog-to-digital converter** (**ADC**), which means that it can read voltages from 0V to 5V and map them into integer values between 0 and 1,023 (2^{10} = 1,024). Analog signals are generally used to read data from analog sensors.

A digital signal is a binary signal, which means that it has only two possible values: 0 or 1, high or low. This kind of signal is mostly used to identify or change on and off states, for example, turning an LED bulb on or off.

Edge computing

Devices are also capable of handling some actions by themselves. This could either be a simple decision: for example, if the moisture level of the soil is below 50%, open the water valve for a minute and check the moisture level again after five minutes.

Alternatively, it can be a complex task: for example, determining whether an object detected by the camera of an autonomous car is a person waiting to cross the street or a tree.

Devices that have to process these kinds of analyses cannot always rely on a network or an application for information or assistance. What if one of them is out of service? This could cause an accident.

Therefore, such devices are provided with a different type of capability called edge computing, which is the capability of processing analytics at the very edge of the solution: the device itself. Basically, edge computing allows the device to perform some actions and calculations "offline," without an active connection to a network.

When selecting the device or devices that will be part of your IoT solution, the best method is to ensure that all capabilities are present in the device.

Since there is a very high number of devices in an IoT network, exceeding capabilities can lead to different problems related to cost, power supply, connection protocol, user experience or even solution complexity.

Networking

Another important element of any IoT solution is networking. Today there are several ways to connect devices, so this is an important aspect that has to be considered when choosing your device. The most common networking standards used today are cabled networks or Wi-Fi, cellular/mobile, **LPWAN**, and **LoRa**. All of these have pros and cons, so let's take a closer look at their uses.

Wireless (Wi-Fi) or cabled network

Wi-Fi is the most common standard communication model on the internet. It assumes that the device or object being connected to is capable of connecting to an IEEE 802.x network and therefore is able to handle IP-based networks.

There are many wi-fi capable devices available in the market. Some examples of Wi-Fi modules are the **ExpressIf ESP-8266** and **ESP-32** modules, **Texas Instruments CC3200**, **Microchip ATSAMW25**, **Intel Edison**, and **Galileo**. This is not the complete list of devices and there are many other combinations that combine a Wi-Fi capable controller and an MCU.

Wi-Fi modules are relatively cheap and are generally good options for when it's possible or desirable to use an available network and support high-payload transfers, given their reliability and connection speed (up to 6.7 Gbps).

A Wi-Fi-based IoT solution looks pretty much like the following diagram:

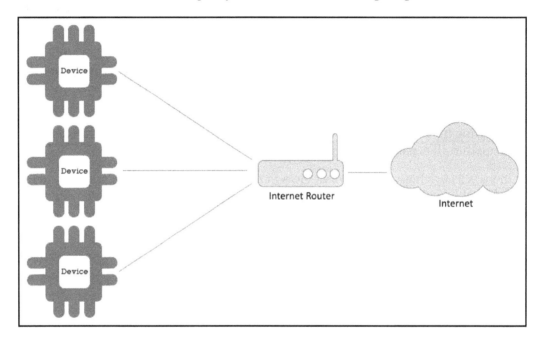

Multiple devices can connect to a node, such as a router, which in turn connects to the internet and allows connected devices to access the internet.

Cellular/mobile network

A cellular network is the same connection that any mobile phone uses. The basic idea with this kind of network is to divide a territory into a number of cells, each one with a wireless network connection served by a base station and a number of transceivers. The network provides a number of services, such as voice, text, and data.

Mobile networks are an option when a device type in a solution is not in the range of a Wi-Fi network, such as in a car. Another application that may require a mobile network device is when the solution cannot depend on the user's network, for example, if you are using a subscription for the device, and the device's activity depends on a network connection. When using the subscription network, the device will continue to do its job even if the user disables their own connection to the network.

The image below depicts the working of a standard cellular network:

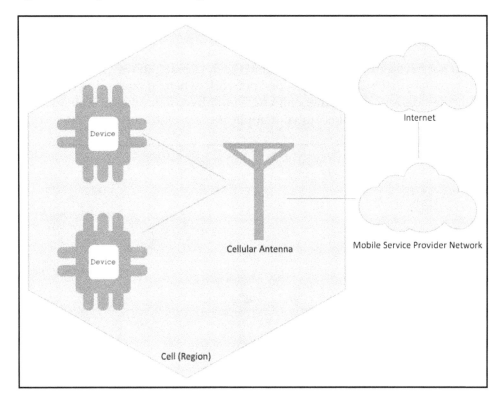

We can see that a cellular antenna provides a signal to a limited region. The devices in range can then connect through a wireless network to the antenna and use the services provided by the mobile service provider, including the available internet connection.

Low-power wide-area network (LPWAN)

LPWAN is a type of wireless network designed to work in wide areas at very low bitrates, which means that the exchange in this type of network is really small.

LPWAN uses low-power, low-bitrate, and low-frequency devices that are very powerful when used to connect to things. This is because it enables the use of long-lasting batteries and smaller devices. But there are still many restrictions, such as small data payloads or a limited number of messages per day.

Having lower frequencies allows an LPWAN to be very reliable and unsusceptible to interference, even when propagating messages for very large ranges. LPWAN providers normally have a limit for the number of messages sent in the network. There are many providers of LPWANs, and the most famous of these is probably Sigfox.

LPWANs do not have a direct connection from the device or gateway to the internet. Instead, they usually have a pre-provisioned network, where at one end of the network you will have the devices and at the other end you would have a number of web hooks and functions that allow you to connect to your application or platform:

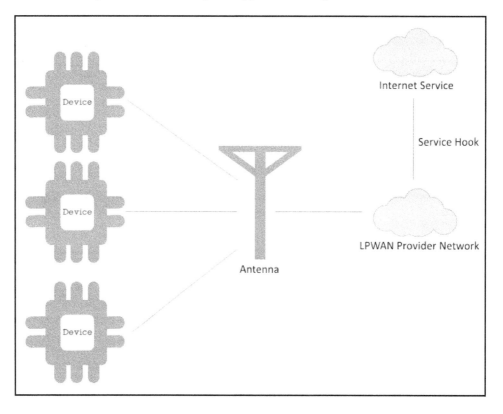

Different from a cellular network, LPWAN networks do not provide internet connection to the devices, instead they provide means to create triggers on events received from the devices to the network. As an example, you can create an application and a trigger at the edge of the LPWAN provider network to the internet that whenever a data event is received from a device, it calls a service available at the internet with given data from the even published by the device.

LoRa or LoRaWAN

A LoRa network diagram is similar to an LPWAN network, except that instead of using service provider infrastructure, LoRa networks can have a gateway that allows devices to connect to the internet. The person responsible for a LoRa network infrastructure is the owner of the network, meaning that you do not rely on a network service provider. You create your own network:

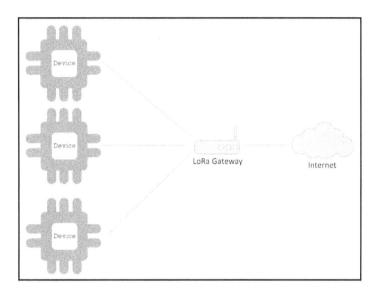

There are a few technologies that work on the same model as LoRA, with different protocols, such as ZigBee. Phillips Hue uses the same approach to connect light bulbs, LED stripes, and other Hue devices to a gateway using ZigBee, and the gateway then connects to the Hue cloud.

Network summary

To summarize, you can use this table as a reference when selecting network connections:

Type	Speed	Payload	Range	Connection initialization	Cost	Infrastructure
Wi-Fi	High	High	Low	Bidirectional	Low	Private/Public
Mobile	High	High	High	Bidirectional	High	Provider
LPWAN	Low	Low	High	Device	Low	Provider
LoRa	Low	Low	High	Bidirectional	Low	Private

Application protocols

After deciding the most adequate device for your IoT solution, it's important to define the protocol that will be used to communicate with devices. IoT solutions tend to use lightweight protocols, such as MQTT. This is not the only protocol that can be used in IoT, but since the IBM Watson IoT Platform relies on MQTT and REST—and REST is very popular—let's focus a little on MQTT.

MQTT

MQTT stands for **Message Queuing Telemetry Transport**. It is an extremely lightweight messaging protocol based on the publish and subscribe pattern. As with any message queuing model, it is an asynchronous protocol.

As shown in the following diagram, publish and subscribe (pub/sub) models rely on three actors:

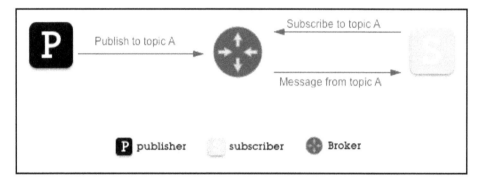

The three actors are explained as follows:

- The **publisher** is the actor that produces any content and publishes it to a given subject (known as a topic).
- The **subscriber** is an event consumer. The subscriber subscribes to its subjects (topics) of interest and gets the event published every time a **publisher** creates a publication to one of its subscriptions.
- The **Broker** is responsible for receiving publications and notifying the subscribers of a topic of interest.

Now let's move on to the next important technical element.

Analytics and AI

Having an analytics or artificial intelligence software component in your IoT solution is not required, but it's really interesting to use them to process data collected from devices to extract patterns and insights that could lead to predictive maintenance, a better understanding of user behavior, and so on.

For example, let's look at some data that is captured through washing machines. Someone may have bought the appliance because it was supposed to save energy. However, after processing the data collected, it becomes clear that the appliance is consuming more energy than thought. The root cause is the lubricant as it was inadequate for its motor in non-tropical countries.

Later, let's say you compare that information with sales data and realize that 1 million washing machines were sold in Europe approximately eight months ago. The manufacturer of the washing machine can get the benefit of early shipping rates for the spare parts that must be exchanged. The manufacturer can also get a predictable amount of new lubricant for their supplier, and this could perhaps lead to a new appliance design.

IBM Watson IoT Platform features

The IBM Watson IoT Platform is a hub for connecting devices, gateways, and applications for IoT solutions. It supports REST and MQTT protocols for applications, devices, gateways, event processing, and administrative tasks. The IBM Watson IoT Platform is available on the IBM Cloud platform (formerly IBM Bluemix), a cloud platform based on Cloud Foundry and Kubernetes.

Let's review the pertinent features of this platform.

Features

In this section, we will discuss the following main features of the IBM Watson IoT Platform:

- Dashboard
- Devices, gateways, and applications,
- Security

Let's begin!

Dashboard

This is the first thing that you will see when you access the IBM Watson IoT Platform. This dashboard can be a combination a number of boards and cards, offering several visualization options for your IoT solution:

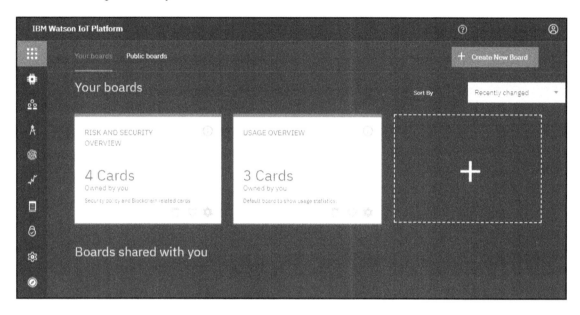

Explore the boards and cards available in this screen to get familiar with the interface.

Devices, gateways, and applications

Another feature available in the platform is device management control. This feature makes it possible to create and remove devices, gateways, applications, and device types. It also makes it possible to check and trigger actions to the device, such as a firmware upgrade request or reset:

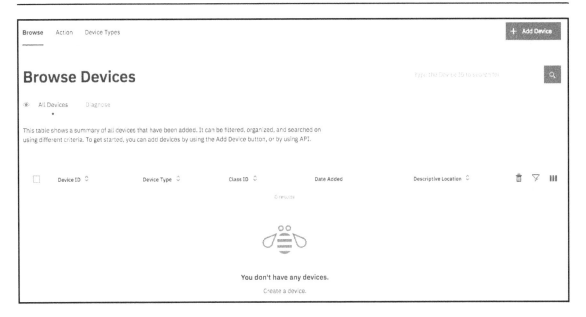

You can also create API keys so that your applications can connect to the IoT organization and interact with the other components of the solution.

Security

You can also manage the security aspects of a solution using the IoT Platform. This might include creating policies for device connections, white and black lists for the device's IP address, or looking at a country's rules. You can also manage users that are permitted or blocked from managing the IoT organization for solutions.

Creating your first IoT solution

In earlier sections of this chapter, there were many devices and applications that were not explained in depth. To understand their roles in an IoT solution, it's important to create one example of each.

The scenario created here will be a **Device** connected to the **IBM Watson IoT Platform** that sends a timestamp as data, as well as an **Application** that prints that to **stdout** using Node.js:

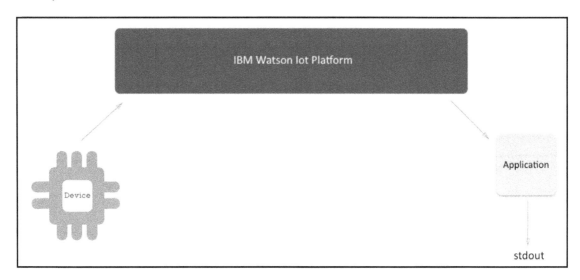

We will then improve this by adding a gateway to the solution, which looks similar to the following diagram:

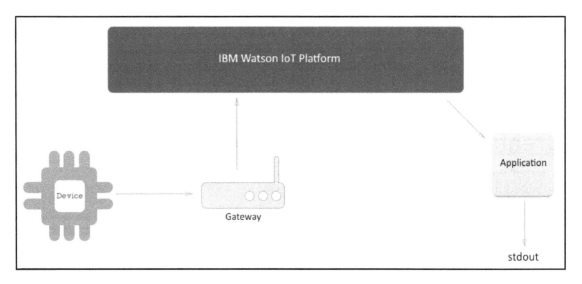

At the end of the day, the difference of having a gateway connection and a device connection is that you can create an abstraction or specialization of the device connected to the IoT platform, depending on whatever is easier, cheaper, or any other reasons that might drive the decision.

Creating a gateway

The first task of the job is to create an IoT organization. If you do not have an IBM ID and IBM Cloud account, the sign-up process is very intuitive and only takes a couple of minutes. If you already have an IBM Cloud account and an IBM ID, access the IBM Cloud platform at `http://bluemix.net`. First, log in and create a space for the exercises in this book.

After logging in to the IBM Cloud platform and accessing the designated space, select the **Create resource** option to access the service catalog:

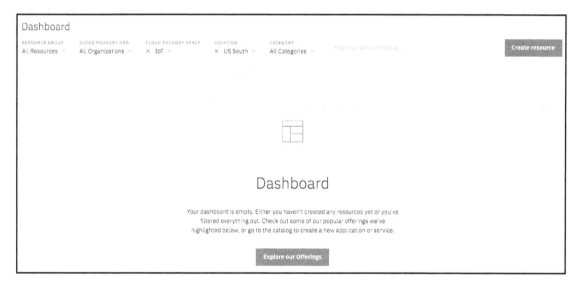

Select **Internet of Things** in the menu and create a service called **Internet of Things Platform**. Now, select the option to **Create:**

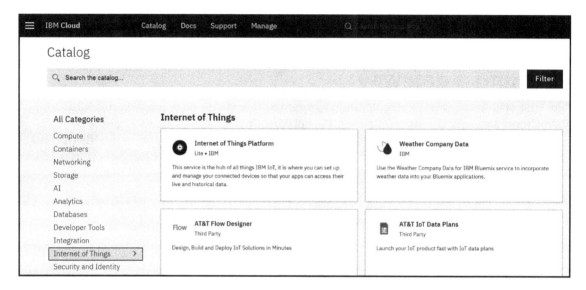

When the service is created, you can select the **Launch** option and access the IoT Platform:

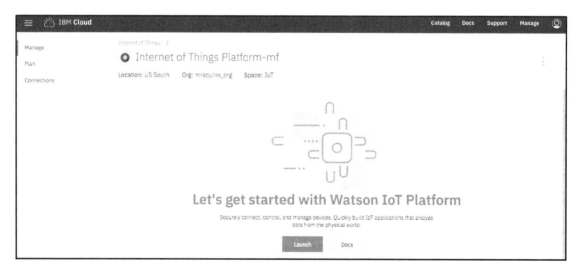

When you access the IoT Platform, notice that the address is
`https://xxxxxx.internetofthings.ibmcloud.com/`.

Here, `xxxxxx` is your organization ID; make a note of it as it will be used during the entire process.

Creating an application

Creating an application means that you're allowing an actual application or service to connect to a specific Watson IoT Platform organization:

1. In order to do that, access the IoT organization through the IBM Cloud dashboard, select Apps from the side menu, then select **Generate API key** and fill in the **Description** field with `Hands-On IoT Solutions with Blockchain - Chapter 1 App`. Finally, click on **Next:**

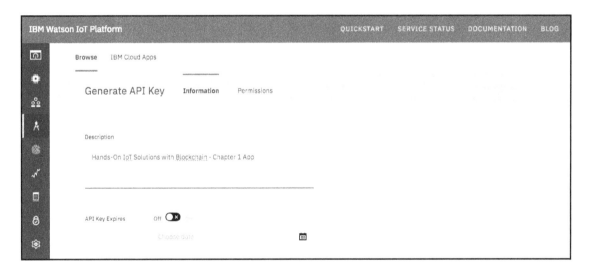

2. Select the **Standard Application** role and click on **Generate Key**. You will get an `API Key` and `Authentication Token`. Make a note of these in a table format, like the one that follows, as you'll need them to connect to your application:

API key	Authentication token

3. Next, open the IDE of your preference, create a new Node.js project, and install the `ibmiotf` dependency package:

```
npm install ibmiotf --save
```

4. Ensure that your `package.json` file looks something like the following:

```
{
  "name": "sample-application",
  "version": "1.0.0",
  "description": "Hands-On IoT Solutions with Blockchain - Chapter
1 App",
  "main": "index.js",
  "scripts": {
    "start": "node .",
    "test": "echo \"Error: no test specified\" && exit 1"
  },
  "author": "Maximiliano Santos",
  "license": "ISC",
  "dependencies": {
    "ibmiotf": "^0.2.41"
  }
}
```

5. Now, create a file named `application.json` with the following content:

```
{
  "org": "<your iot org id>",
  "id": "<any application name>",
  "auth-key": "<application authentication key>",
  "auth-token": "<application authentication token>"
}
```

6. Create a file named `index.js` and add the following content:

```
var Client = require("ibmiotf");
var appClientConfig = require("./application.json");

var appClient = new Client.IotfApplication(appClientConfig);

appClient.connect();

appClient.on("connect", function () {
  console.log("connected");
});
```

7. The application can be tested by running the `npm start` command:

```
$ npm start
> sample-application@1.0.0 start /sample-application
> node .
connected
```

Congratulations, you just created your first application connected to IBM Watson IoT Platform!

8. Now, update `index.js` to have the following content:

```
var Client = require("ibmiotf");
var appClientConfig = require("./application.json");

var appClient = new Client.IotfApplication(appClientConfig);

appClient.connect();

appClient.on("connect", function () {
  appClient.subscribeToDeviceEvents();
});

appClient.on("deviceEvent", function (deviceType, deviceId,
payload, topic) {
    console.log("Device events from : " + deviceType + " : " +
deviceId + " with payload : " + payload);
});
```

Now, whenever a device publishes an event, you will get the event printed to `stdout`. In the next section, we will create a device to publish the events.

Creating a device

In this section, you'll run through similar steps to create a fake device that connects to IBM Watson IoT Platform and publishes an event.

1. From the IoT Platform service created in the setup step, select **Devices** in the menu and then select **Add Device**. Create a device type named **DeviceSimulator** and fill in the **Device ID** field with `DeviceSimulator01`:

2. Since it's only a simulator, just click on **Next** until you reach the end of the wizard:

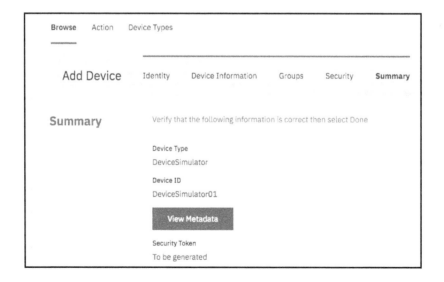

3. Note the device credentials generated, in the following format:

Device type	Device ID	Authentication method	Authentication token

4. Go back to your preferred IDE and create the project with the same characteristics as the previous application:

```
npm install ibmiotf --save
```

5. Ensure that your package.json file looks like the following:

```
{
  "name": "sample-device",
  "version": "1.0.0",
  "description": "Hands-On IoT Solutions with Blockchain - Chapter
1 Device",
  "main": "index.js",
  "scripts": {
    "start": "node .",
    "test": "echo \"Error: no test specified\" && exit 1"
  },
  "author": "Maximiliano Santos",
  "license": "ISC",
  "dependencies": {
    "ibmiotf": "^0.2.41"
  }
}
```

6. Then, create a file named device.json with the following content:

```
{
  "org": "<your iot org id>",
  "type": "DeviceSimulator",
  "id": "DeviceSimulator01",
  "auth-method" : "token",
  "auth-token" : "<device authentication token>"
}
```

7. Create a file named `index.js` and add the following content:

```
var iotf = require("ibmiotf");
var config = require("./device.json");

var deviceClient = new iotf.IotfDevice(config);

deviceClient.log.setLevel('debug');

deviceClient.connect();

deviceClient.on('connect', function(){
  console.log("connected");
});
```

8. The device simulator can be tested by running the `npm start` command:

```
$ npm start
> sample-device@1.0.0 start /sample-device
> node .
[BaseClient:connect] Connecting to IoTF with host :
ssl://3nr17i.messaging.internetofthings.ibmcloud.co
m:8883 and with client id :
d:3nr17i:DeviceSimulator:DeviceSimulator01
[DeviceClient:connect] DeviceClient Connected
connected
```

9. Now, update the code to send an event with the current timestamp to the IoT Platform service:

```
var iotf = require("ibmiotf");
var config = require("./device.json");

var deviceClient = new iotf.IotfDevice(config);

deviceClient.log.setLevel('debug');

deviceClient.connect();

deviceClient.on('connect', function() {
  console.log("connected");
  setInterval(function function_name () {
    deviceClient.publish('myevt', 'json', '{"value":' + new Date()
+'}', 2);
  },2000);
});
```

10. Run `npm start` again and every two seconds the device will send an event to the Watson IoT Platform. You can check the logs of the application to see whether it has received the events, like so:

```
Device Event from :: DeviceSimulator : DeviceSimulator01 of event
myevt with payload : {"value":Sun May 20 2018 21:55:19 GMT-0300
(-03)}
Device Event from :: DeviceSimulator : DeviceSimulator01 of event
myevt with payload : {"value":Sun May 20 2018 21:55:21 GMT-0300
(-03)}
Device Event from :: DeviceSimulator : DeviceSimulator01 of event
myevt with payload : {"value":Sun May 20 2018 21:55:23 GMT-0300
(-03)}
Device Event from :: DeviceSimulator : DeviceSimulator01 of event
myevt with payload : {"value":Sun May 20 2018 21:55:25 GMT-0300
(-03)}
```

Congratulations again, your device simulator is now publishing events and your application is receiving them!

Summary

In this chapter, we had an overview of the IoT environment. We learned about some important technical elements that play a role in the successful implementation of an IoT solution.

We also looked at the different types of networking options, important considerations when selecting a device type, and how to create a device and an application connected to the IBM Watson IoT Platform.

In the next chapter, you will improve your development skills by creating a simple connected garden.

Further reading

Examples in other languages such as Python, Java, C++, and C# can be found in the IBM Watson IoT Platform documentation at the following link: `https://console.bluemix.net/docs/services/IoT/getting-started.html#getting-started-with-iotp`.

Creating Your First IoT Solution

In the previous chapter, we explored the **Internet of Things** (**IoT**) as well as the IBM Watson IoT Platform. We also created our first simple solution. In this chapter, we will put this into practice by creating a simple end-to-end solution, from selecting the device to creating the device firmware and an application designed to control a simple garden watering system.

The following topics will be covered in this chapter:

- Understanding how to set up a solution
- Creating a connected device
- Creating a simple application connected to the platform
- Publishing and processing device events
- Publishing actions to devices
- How to get help when you're in trouble

Technical requirements

The complete solution code is available in the `ch2` folder, available at the `https://github.com/PacktPublishing/Hands-On-IoT-Solutions-with-Blockchain.git` repository.

Make sure that you have also installed Cloud Foundry CLI and Bluemix CLI; the installation process for these command-line interfaces is described at `https://console.bluemix.net/docs/cli/index.html#overview`.

The first IoT solution – the gardening solution

Watering systems are common first projects for using IoT in the DIY community. We too will use it as an example project to get started on the IBM Watson IoT Platform.

Requirements overview

Good solutions are based on problems that really matter to people. So let's start our solution with an introduction to the actual problem:

John lives alone in an apartment in the city. He is a businessman who has to travel for work for 3-4 days in a week. When not travelling or working, John likes to take care of his plants. However, since he is not home for half the week, John is struggling to keep his garden healthy and beautiful.

John has faced several challenging experiences with automated watering systems: either the system did not water the plants enough (on hot or dry days, for example), or it watered them too much when the weather was okay.

John is looking for a solution that only waters his garden when a plant has reached a certain soil moisture condition, or whenever he feels it is necessary.

Solution overview

The following diagram shows an overview of the solution components that will be developed to solve John's problem:

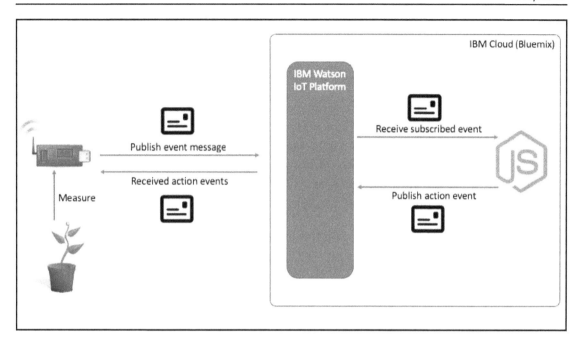

A connected device will be attached to John's plant, and on a scheduled basis will retrieve measurements from the plant and environment (soil moisture and temperature) and publish the event to the IBM Watson IoT Platform. The device will also subscribe to trigger commands (actions).

An application deployed to the IBM Cloud (Bluemix) will subscribe to John's events, and whenever a configured minimum level of soil moisture or a high temperature threshold is reached, the application will send an action command to water the plant for a certain duration.

Selecting the equipment

Given the requirements described in the previous section, the device that needs to be created must have the following capabilities:

- Be able to measure the soil's moisture level (an analog probe has a good fit for this solution)
- Have bidirectional communication capability (so that the user can water the garden whenever he feels it is necessary)
- Be able to configure the soil's moisture limit (a configurable rule)

The following assumptions are also true about the solution:

- The user will prov

    - ide a Wi-Fi internet connection
    - The user will provide an energy supply for the system
    - The system will be used in an apartment, so there is no need for long-distance connections
    - Payload size is irr
  - elevant as a Wi-Fi connection will be provided

Since we are prototyping before creating the actual device, there are a number of prototyping platforms that can make it easier to wire and test the solution quickly. To do this, we will use one of the most powerful and modular platforms: Intel Edison and Grove.

We will look for a device (or a composition) that has Wi-Fi connectivity and an analog sensor connection. We will also need a soil moisture analog sensor probe, a temperature and humidity sensor, and a water solenoid valve.

Consequently, the solution will require a list of parts, which will look something like this:

Quantity	Component
1	Intel Edison module
1	Intel Edison Arduino breakout board
1	Grove base shield v2
1	Grove soil moisture sensor
1	Groove temperature sensor v1.2
1	Grove relay module
1	Grove button module
4	Grove universal 4-pin cable
1	12V water solenoid valve
1	12V 2A power supply
2	Jumper cables (male to male)

The following diagram provides an overview of the parts that are specified in the parts list table. Please note that the shape and color of the devices are just for illustration purposes and might be different depending on the vendor, edition, or other characteristics:

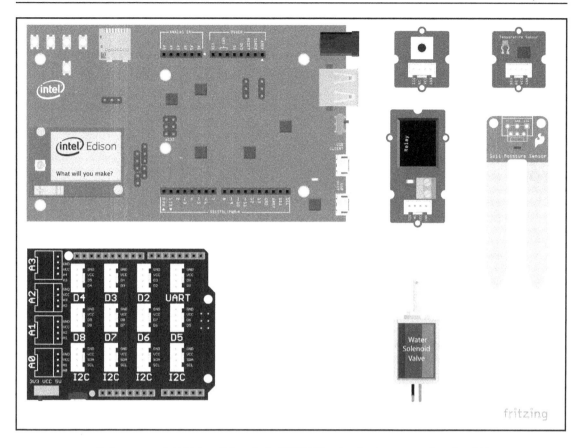

The image was created with Fritzing and is licensed under CC BY-SA 3.0: see https://creativecommons.org/licenses/by-sa/3.0/

Let's quickly review the parts from this list.

Intel Edison

Edison is a **system-on-a-chip** (**SoC**), based on Intel x86 architecture with embedded Bluetooth 4.0 and Wi-Fi designed for IoT applications. Edison runs a Linux distribution named Yocto; has support for many platforms, such as Python, Node.js, C, and C++; and has plugins for developing solutions using Arduino IDE, Eclipse, and Intel XDK.

Arduino breakout board

The Arduino breakout board for Edison was also released by Intel, which provides the same standard pin interface used by Arduino modules and is compatible with Arduino shields. Since you can use the standard Arduino IDE, compatible libraries, connectors, and shields, the Intel Edison Arduino breakout board is a great interface for prototyping and running Arduino sketches.

Grove system

Grove is a set of components and shields that creates a standardized modular platform with building blocks for prototyping solutions created by Seeed. There are many available prototypes, including working code for the Grove platform available on the internet, especially on **do-it-yourself** (**DIY**) community sites.

The Grove system has shields for platforms with heavy adoption in the market, such as Arduino, Raspberry Pi, and BeagleBone. Bundles with the compute module, base shield, Grove blocks, and spare parts can be found on the internet.

Note that not every sensor is compatible with every platform because some platforms lack certain capabilities. For example, Raspberry Pi does not provide analog interfaces, so sensors that are connectable through an analog interface will not be compatible with it.

Let's look at all the Grove components we will use as part of this IoT solution.

Grove base shield for Arduino

In this project, we will use the Grove base shield for Arduino, which provides an interface for Grove standard connectors to connect Grove modules to the Arduino pin interface. It provides four analog interfaces, four I2C interfaces, seven digital interfaces, and a UART interface.

Grove sensors

In this project, we will be using two different types of sensors: the soil moisture sensor and the temperature sensor.

The soil moisture sensor is an analog probe that provides soil resistive measurements, which we will explain later in this chapter. The temperature of the sensor is based on a thermistor, and its specifications and calculation are also detailed later in the *Measuring environment temperature* section.

Both sensors use the standard Grove connector cable that provides VCC, GND, and data connectivity to the probe.

Grove button

This button follows the same connectivity to the computing module as the sensors but provides an open or closed circuit state, depending on whether the button is pressed or not.

It can have different interpretations: either the connection is interrupted when the button is pressed, meaning it will keep doing something unless the button is pressed; or the connection is activated when the button is pressed, meaning it will only do something after the button is pressed.

Grove relay

The relay module, as expected, is connected to the standard Grove interface, but it is classified as an actuator because it does not provide readings.

Other actuator modules such as LEDs, displays, motor drivers, and buzzers are used to perform actions instead of reading states. The relay module too has two states, open circuit or closed circuit, meaning that the input connection of the relay is not connected to the output.

This concludes our review of the parts. Let's move on to the next step in the solution development process.

Wiring the device

To assemble the hardware, we need to correctly connect the sensor probes to the processing unit—in this case, the Intel Edison module.

Grove modules make the connections very simple, as the following steps show:

1. Using the Grove universal cables:
    *   Attach the Grove moisture sensor to the A0 connection jack in the base shield
    *   Attach the Grove temperature sensor to the A3 connection jack in the base shield

- Attach the Grove relay module to the D2 connection jack in the base shield
- Attach the Grove button module to the D3 connection jack in the base shield

2. Using the jumpers:
   - Attach the solenoid valve's V+ end to an external 12V power supply
   - Attach the external GND pin to a GND pin in the base shield
   - Attach a relay connection to a GND pin
   - Attach the solenoid valve GND terminal to the other relay module connection

The following diagram shows the correct connections:

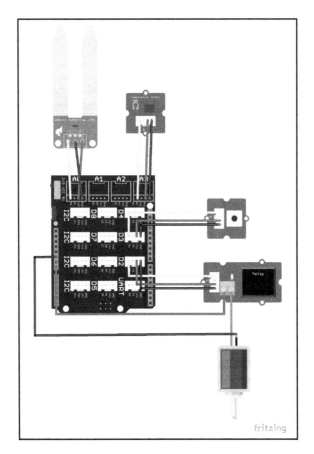

Coding the device firmware

Next, we will create a device application (firmware) that reads the sensor data and sends it to the backing application. In the previous chapter, we used Node.js to publish events from a device simulator, and now we're going to use this method to leverage the previous chapter's code. Remember that the objective of this solution is to water a plant whenever the temperature is high or the soil moisture is too low.

The next section shows the code needed in order to create the firmware that reads all the sensor data and publishes events to the IBM Watson IoT Platform.

Measuring soil moisture

The sensor probe used in this project is a resistive sensor, which measures the current that is passed through the probes of the sensor. It has two probes that are physically separated; one probe is attached to a positive end and the other to the GND end. When both probes are connected by a common surface, it will measure the current that is passed through that surface and give us a reading.

In our case, when the probes touch the soil, it will measure the current that passes through. When soil gets wet, it becomes more conductive, meaning that more current will pass through the probes.

The Intel Edison ADC (analog-to-digital) converter that is in the Arduino breakout board has a 12-bit resolution, but this is limited through software to a 10-bit resolution. If we use this as the basis for our measurement, we will get the following understanding of the readings:

$$2^{10} = 1024$$

This means that our readings will be a value from 0 to 1,023, where 0 means no water at all and 1,023 means 100% of the water. This will vary because of other impurities that are present in the soil, such as minerals. However, in this case, we will assume that the soil is perfectly measured. When it's completely dry, it will give us a measurement of 0% and if it's a glass of water without any soil, it will give us a reading of 100%.

The following code will read the soil moisture sensor every two seconds:

```
var mraa = require('mraa');
var pin0 = new mraa.Aio(0);
var getSoilMoisture = function() {
  var sensorReading = pin0.read();
  return sensorReading;
};
setInterval(function() {
  console.log("Current Moisture " + getSoilMoisture());
},2000);
```

To run the code, type `npm start` in Edison's SSH console.

For testing purposes, let's take a look at the measurement readings of the sensors that are printed to the console and gain some understanding of the values:

```
[root@edison-iot:~/iot# npm start

> iot@1.0.0 start /home/root/iot
> node .

Current moisture 256
Current moisture 307
Current moisture 302
Current moisture 303
Current moisture 299
Current moisture 298
Current moisture 304
Current moisture 301
Current moisture 306
Current moisture 301
Current moisture 305
Current moisture 305
Current moisture 301
Current moisture 302
Current moisture 304
Current moisture 305
Current moisture 300
```

We already know that 0 means 0% water and 1,023 is 100, which means that the sample measurement readings in the program are as follows:

$$Percent = \frac{reading}{highest\ value} \times 100 \quad \text{or} \quad Percent = \frac{reading}{1023} \times 100$$

Applying the reading values to the preceding formula will transform them into percentage values as follows:

Reading values	Moisture percentage
256	25.02%
307	30.00%
302	29.52%
303	29.61%
299	29.22%
298	29.13%

Measuring environmental temperature

Similar to the previous code block (but slightly more mathematically complicated), the temperature sensor returns an analog reading of the sensor.

If we look at the manufacturer's explanation (`http://wiki.seeedstudio.com/Grove-Temperature_Sensor_V1.2/`) on how to read the sensor, we will discover that the sensor's v1.2 is shipped with a thermistor with the value of 4,250 as well as a 100k resistor.

Consequently, the formula for calculating the temperature value using this sensor is as follows:

$$Temperature = \cfrac{1}{\cfrac{\log\left(\cfrac{\cfrac{1023}{(SensorReading - 1 \times ResistorValue)}}{ResistorValue}\right)}{ThermistorValue + 1}} - 273.15$$

The following code will give the temperature based on the sensor readings every two seconds:

```
var mraa = require('mraa');
var pin3 = new mraa.Aio(3);
var RESISTOR = 100000;
var THERMISTOR = 4250;
var getTemperature = function() {
  var sensorReading = pin3.read();
  var R = 1023 / sensorReading - 1;
  R = RESISTOR * R;
  var temperature = 1 / (Math.log(R/RESISTOR)/THERMISTOR+1/298.15)-273.15;
```

```
  return temperature;
};
setInterval(function() {
  console.log("Current Temperature " + getTemperature());
},2000);
```

The output of this code will look something like this:

```
[root@edison-iot:~/iot# npm start

> iot@1.0.0 start /home/root/iot
> node .

Current Temperature 11.675092536719035
Current Temperature 10.923006601697807
Current Temperature 11.006864299358028
Current Temperature 11.090646733903895
Current Temperature 11.425042046824103
Current Temperature 10.923006601697807
Current Temperature 11.090646733903895
Current Temperature 11.25798946566158
Current Temperature 11.425042046824103
```

Using the SSH console, these readings will be logged.

Turning on the relay

Last but not least, since we want to turn on a relay that will let water flow and then turn it off, the code for turning the water on after one second and off after two seconds is as follows:

```
var mraa = require('mraa');
var pinD2 = new mraa.Gpio(2);
pinD2.dir(mraa.DIR_OUT);
setTimeout(function() {
  pinD2.write(1);
  setTimeout(function() {
    pinD2.write(0);
  },2000);
},1000);
```

After a delay of one second, you'll see the `D3` relay module LED turn on and you will also hear a click. This means that the relay connection is closed, and after two seconds it will turn off and open the connection.

Publishing events

At this point in the chapter, we have explored Node.js scripts that are capable of reading both soil moisture and temperatures, and we have also looked at the code that can turn on and turn off the relay that lets the water flow to the plant.

The goal is now to publish both of these values to the IBM Watson IoT Platform.

As shown in the previous chapter, it's necessary to create a device and note the credentials, so that we can use them to connect the device to the platform. The following code performs the regular publishing of the events:

```
var iotf = require("ibmiotf");
var mraa = require('mraa');
var config = require("./device.json");
var deviceClient = new iotf.IotfDevice(config);
var temperatureSensor = new mraa.Aio(3);
var moistureSensor = new mraa.Aio(0);
var RESISTOR = 100000;
var THERMISTOR = 4250;
var getTemperature = function() {
 var sensorReading = temperatureSensor.read();
 var R = 1023 / sensorReading - 1;
 R = RESISTOR * R;
 var temperature = 1 / (Math.log(R/RESISTOR)/THERMISTOR+1/298.15)-273.15;
 return temperature;
};
var getSoilMoisture = function() {
 var sensorReading = moistureSensor.read();
 return sensorReading;
};
deviceClient.connect();
deviceClient.on('connect', function(){
console.log("connected");
setInterval(function function_name () {
deviceClient.publish('status', 'json', '{ "temperature": ' +
getTemperature() +', "soilMoisture": ' + getSoilMoisture() + '}', 2);
},300000);
});
```

When the scripts start, they will load the configuration from the `device.json` file, connect to the IBM Watson IoT Platform, and then publish an event with the current soil moisture and temperature every five minutes.

Monitoring the events

The easiest way to view the data published by the device is by using boards and cards. If you keep the device script running when creating the card, it will get the values from the data structure published by the device.

1. To create a card, access the **IBM Watson IoT Platform** console and select boards in the left menu:

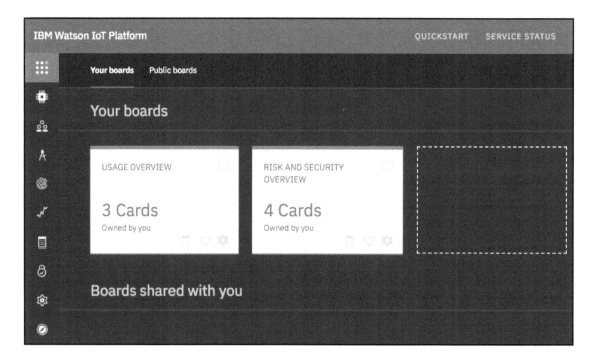

2. At the top right of the page, select **+ Create New Board**, complete the information
   required, and create the board. Most information that must be provided is
   miscellaneous, but make sure it is meaningful to the target user. The board
   created here is supposed to display the plants monitored readings:

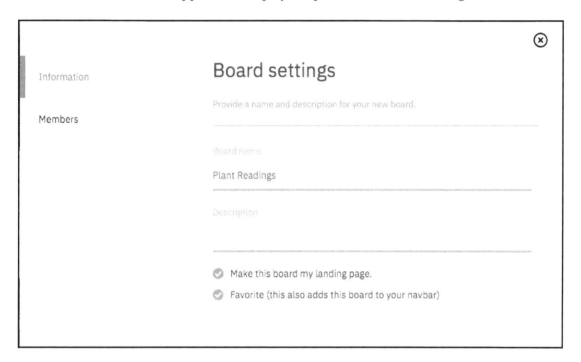

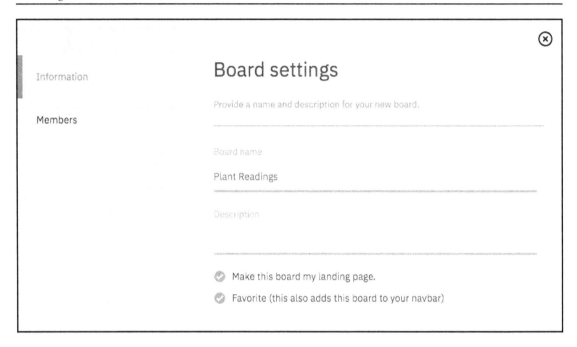

A board is a set of related cards, and a card is a set of related values that were published by devices to the platform.

3. Select the created board and create the card by selecting **+ Add New Card.**

4. Select the **Line chart** device visualization and the device created:

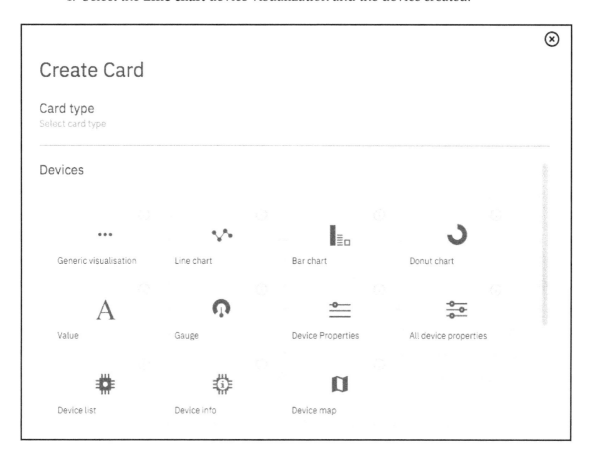

5. After selecting **Line chart** card, you need to select a data source for the event. Select the device created as the data source for this card. The data source, as the name says, is the source of information that will be used to populate the chart with metrics collected from devices:

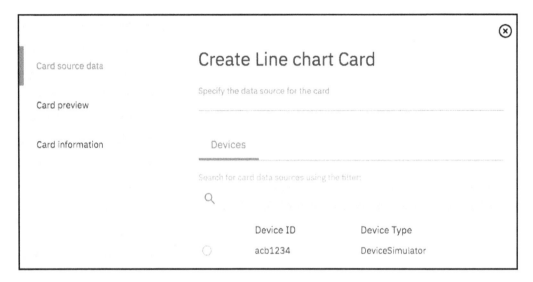

6. After selecting the data source, it's necessary to select the metrics that will be plotted on the chart. If the device has already published some events to the IBM Watson IoT Platform, the metric names will be available to be selected. On the other hand, if the device code has never been run before, you will need to provide the metric names. It's recommended (not required) that you at least test the device code to avoid mistakes before creating the chart.

7. In the solution that is being developed, we want the card to have both metrics plotted in the line chart and tracked. Add each metric with its corresponding unit and maximum and minimum possible values. For the soil moisture, we use percentage, so **Unit** should be % for the minimum and maximum values 0 and 100 respectively:

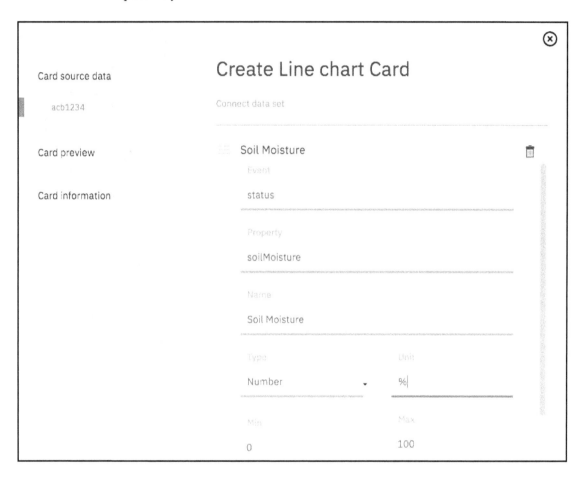

8. For temperature, measured in degrees Celsius (°C), the minimum and maximum possible values are 0 and 100:

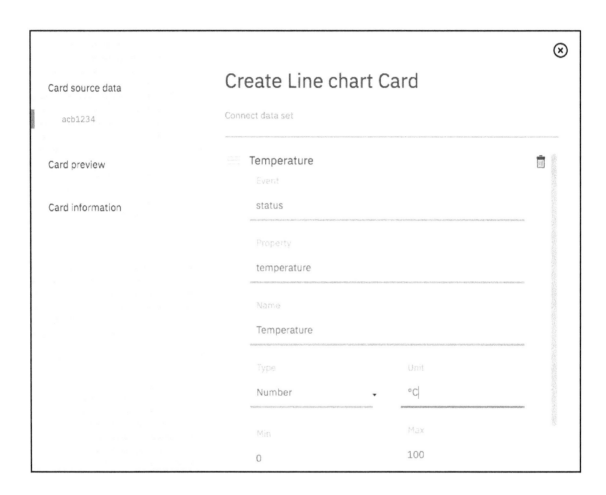

9. Select the size of the card you prefer to display, name the card, and create it. You will now be able to visualize the published data:

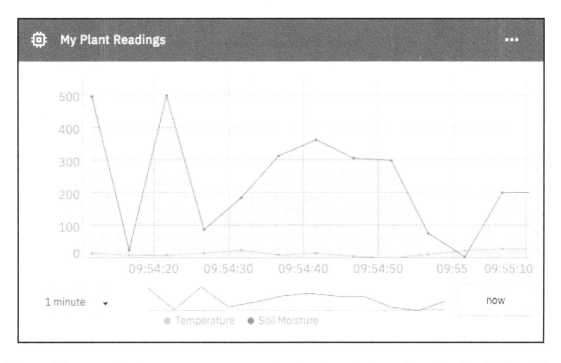

It's possible to verify the measurements sent by the plant device, plotted in the timeline. It's also possible to change the time frame for the chart.

Subscribing to actions

After publishing events for the device, it's time to define actions that need to be handled by the device. In our case, John, the user of the solution, wants to be able to water his plants whenever a defined soil moisture threshold is detected, whenever the temperature reaches a configurable value, or whenever he triggers an event to water the plant.

The water flow is controlled by the solenoid valve, which is opened and closed by the relay module. The following code is an update of the previous one, including the subscription for the water-the-plant action, which will open the valve for a minute.

1. The starting point is to import all package dependencies, define the `RESISTOR` and `THERMISTOR` constants with predefined values, and load the configuration from `device.json`:

```
var iotf = require("ibmiotf");
var mraa = require('mraa');
var config = require("./device.json");
var deviceClient = new iotf.IotfDevice(config);
var temperatureSensor = new mraa.Aio(3);
var moistureSensor = new mraa.Aio(0);
var relayControl = new mraa.Gpio(2);
var RESISTOR = 100000;
var THERMISTOR = 4250;
```

2. Then, create helper functions to transform sensor readings into usable values. The following functions are responsible for retrieving the sensor values from the actual device and transforming them into human-understandable values:

```
var getTemperature = function() {
  var sensorReading = temperatureSensor.read();
  var R = 1023 / sensorReading - 1;
  R = RESISTOR * R;
  var temperature = 1 /
(Math.log(R/RESISTOR)/THERMISTOR+1/298.15)-273.15;
  return temperature;
};
var getSoilMoisture = function() {
  var sensorReading = moistureSensor.read();
  return sensorReading;
};
```

3. The next step is to create a helper function to activate the solenoid valve, wait for the amount of time requested (the `secondsToWater` variable's value), and then deactivate the valve so watering will stop:

```
var waterPlant = function(secondsToWater) {
  relayControl.write(1);
  setTimeout(function() {
    pinD2.write(0);
  },secondsToWater * 1000);
```

4. Connect to the IBM Watson IoT Platform and create a publishing function that will publish events to the platform every five minutes:

```
deviceClient.connect();
deviceClient.on('connect', function(){
  console.log("connected");
```

```
setInterval(function function_name () {
    deviceClient.publish('status', 'json', '{ "temperature": ' +
getTemperature() +', "soilMoisture": ' + getSoilMoisture() + '}',
2);
    },300000);
});
```

5. And create a function that subscribes to the `water` event, triggering the
   `waterPlant` function:

```
deviceClient.on("command", function
(commandName,format,payload,topic) {
  if(commandName === "water") {
    var commandPayload = JSON.parse(payload.toString());
    console.log("Watering the plant for " + commandPayload.duration
+ " seconds.");
    waterPlant(commandPayload.duration);
  } else {
    console.log("Command not supported.. " + commandName);
  }
});
```

This concludes the coding of our device firmware so that it can perform the desired actions
of our user, John.

Creating the backend application

With the device firmware setup completed, it's now time to focus on developing the
application that will process the device events and send commands so that John's plant will
get watered when he's not home.

The code for the application will run on the IBM Cloud Platform (Bluemix). Since this is just
an example application, we're going to use environment variables to store parameters
(temperature and soil moisture thresholds).

Creating a Cloud Foundry application in the IBM Cloud Platform

1. To create an application in IBM Cloud, access `https://console.bluemix.net`, select the **Create Resource** option, and select **Cloud Foundry Apps** in the left menu, followed by SDK for Node.js. After doing this, name the application and create the runtime:

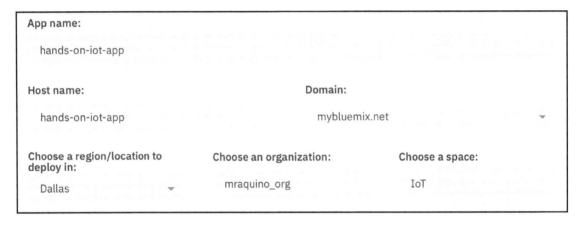

2. When application creation is complete, select **Connections** in the left menu and create a connection to the IoT service:

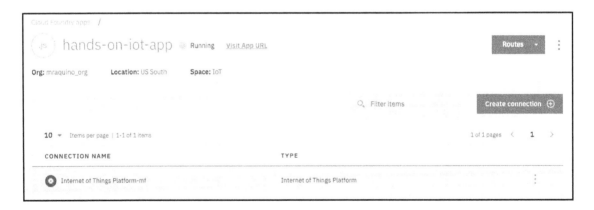

3. After creating the connection to the IBM Watson IoT Platform organization, select the **Runtime** option in the left menu followed by **Environment Variables.** At the bottom of the screen, add two **User defined** variables, MINIMUM_MOISTURE with a value of 300 and MAXIMUM_TEMPERATURE with a value of 50:

User defined		
NAME	VALUE	ACTION
MINIMUM_MOISTURE	300	⊗
MAXIMUM_TEMPERATURE	50	⊗

Instead of using a JSON file for storing the configuration as we did in the previous chapter, the only configuration needed now is in VCAP_SERVICES and environment variables. These variables can be accessed from code using default library packages, and there are accelerators in Node.js for accessing Cloud Foundry environment-related facilities, such as the cfenv module used in the code presented in the following section.

Uploading the code

Since we are deploying the application to a Cloud Foundry environment, it's important to know that Cloud Foundry containers expect to have an HTTP port to be published by the container, so even though we are not using the container to expose HTTP resources, we're going to start an Express JS server.

The following code handles the events received from devices and publishes actions if any conditions are met.

1. Again, the entry point of the code is to load module dependencies and gather the required configuration from the Cloud Foundry environment variables:

```
var express = require("express");
var cfenv = require("cfenv");
var Client = require("ibmiotf");
var minimumMoisture = parseInt(process.env.MINIMUM_MOISTURE);
var maximumTemperature = parseInt(process.env.MAXIMUM_TEMPERATURE);
```

2. Then, load configuration data from the Cloud Foundry environment and generate connection configuration data:

```
var app = express();
```

```
var appEnv = cfenv.getAppEnv();
var iotConfig = appEnv.getService("Internet of Things Platform-
mf");
var appClientConfig = {
  "org": iotConfig.credentials.org,
  "id": "hands-on-iot-app",
  "auth-key": iotConfig.credentials.apiKey,
  "auth-token": iotConfig.credentials.apiToken
}
```

3. The next step is to connect to the IBM Watson IoT Platform and subscribe to target device events:

```
var appClient = new Client.IotfApplication(appClientConfig);
appClient.connect();
appClient.on("connect", function () {
  appClient.subscribeToDeviceEvents();
});
appClient.on("deviceEvent", function (deviceType, deviceId,
eventType, format, payload) {
  var deviceData = JSON.parse(payload);
```

4. Whenever an event is received from the subscription, the application checks whether the temperature reported by the device is higher or the soil moisture is below the thresholds defined. If so, a water event with a specified duration in seconds is published to the device so the watering valve is activated:

```
if(deviceData.temperature > maximumTemperature ||
deviceData.soilMoisture < minimumMoisture ) {
    console.log("Device, please water the plant for 60 seconds");
    var actionData= { duration : 60 };
    actionData = JSON.stringify(actionData);
    appClient.publishDeviceCommand(deviceType, deviceId, "water",
"json", actionData);
  }
});
```

5. And finally, start the Express server so the IBM Cloud SDK for Node.js container is started and monitored by the Cloud Foundry environment:

```
var port = process.env.PORT;
app.listen(port, function() {
 console.log("App listening!");
});
```

To deploy the application, open the `manifest.yml` file and change the `name` attribute of the application. Then, open a command-line terminal, switch to the application base directory (the place where `manifest.yml` stands), and deploy the application using the `bluemix` CLI:

```
bluemix login

bluemix target -o <your_cloud_foundry_organization_name> -s
<space_where_your_app_will_be_deployed>

bluemix cf push
```

```
Waiting for app to start...

name:               hands-on-iot-app
requested state:    started
instances:          1/1
usage:              256M x 1 instances
routes:             hands-on-iot-app.mybluemix.net
last uploaded:      Fri 29 Jun 15:04:15 -03 2018
stack:              cflinuxfs2
buildpack:          SDK for Node.js(TM) (ibm-node.js-6.13.0, buildpack-v3.20.2-20180524-2057)
start command:      ./vendor/initial_startup.rb

     state    since                 cpu    memory         disk          details
#0   running  2018-06-29T18:06:02Z  0.0%   71.5M of 256M  86.1M of 1G
```

After getting the successful deployment message, check the application logs using the `bluemix` CLI:

```
bluemix cf logs <your_application_name>
```

The command will retrieve and display the log files from the Cloud Foundry application, as shown next. To ensure you can retrieve these logs, ensure that all application traces are being sent to `stdout` and `stderr`:

```
Invoking 'cf logs hands-on-iot-app'...

Retrieving logs for app hands-on-iot-app in org              / space IoT as mraquino@br.ibm.com...

2018-06-29T15:27:42.40-0300 [APP/PROC/WEB/0] OUT Device Event from :: DeviceSimulator : acb1234 of event status with payload : { "temperature": 28, "soilMoisture": 148}
2018-06-29T15:27:47.40-0300 [APP/PROC/WEB/0] OUT Device Event from :: DeviceSimulator : acb1234 of event status with payload : { "temperature": 21, "soilMoisture": 257}
2018-06-29T15:27:52.41-0300 [APP/PROC/WEB/0] OUT Device Event from :: DeviceSimulator : acb1234 of event status with payload : { "temperature": 27, "soilMoisture": 21}
2018-06-29T15:27:57.41-0300 [APP/PROC/WEB/0] OUT Device Event from :: DeviceSimulator : acb1234 of event status with payload : { "temperature": 20, "soilMoisture": 321}
2018-06-29T15:28:02.41-0300 [APP/PROC/WEB/0] OUT Device Event from :: DeviceSimulator : acb1234 of event status with payload : { "temperature": 4, "soilMoisture": 364}
2018-06-29T15:28:07.41-0300 [APP/PROC/WEB/0] OUT Device Event from :: DeviceSimulator : acb1234 of event status with payload : { "temperature": 4, "soilMoisture": 390}
2018-06-29T15:28:12.42-0300 [APP/PROC/WEB/0] OUT Device Event from :: DeviceSimulator : acb1234 of event status with payload : { "temperature": 18, "soilMoisture": 5}
2018-06-29T15:28:17.42-0300 [APP/PROC/WEB/0] OUT Device Event from :: DeviceSimulator : acb1234 of event status with payload : { "temperature": 20, "soilMoisture": 370}
2018-06-29T15:28:22.42-0300 [APP/PROC/WEB/0] OUT Device Event from :: DeviceSimulator : acb1234 of event status with payload : { "temperature": 14, "soilMoisture": 156}
2018-06-29T15:28:27.43-0300 [APP/PROC/WEB/0] OUT Device Event from :: DeviceSimulator : acb1234 of event status with payload : { "temperature": 25, "soilMoisture": 418}
2018-06-29T15:28:32.43-0300 [APP/PROC/WEB/0] OUT Device Event from :: DeviceSimulator : acb1234 of event status with payload : { "temperature": 27, "soilMoisture": 85}
2018-06-29T15:28:37.43-0300 [APP/PROC/WEB/0] OUT Device Event from :: DeviceSimulator : acb1234 of event status with payload : { "temperature": 27, "soilMoisture": 437}
2018-06-29T15:28:42.43-0300 [APP/PROC/WEB/0] OUT Device Event from :: DeviceSimulator : acb1234 of event status with payload : { "temperature": 11, "soilMoisture": 227}
2018-06-29T15:28:47.44-0300 [APP/PROC/WEB/0] OUT Device Event from :: DeviceSimulator : acb1234 of event status with payload : { "temperature": 27, "soilMoisture": 376}
2018-06-29T15:28:52.44-0300 [APP/PROC/WEB/0] OUT Device Event from :: DeviceSimulator : acb1234 of event status with payload : { "temperature": 25, "soilMoisture": 15}
```

Log files from the Cloud Foundry application

Looking at the device logs, you can see that whenever any of the conditions were met, they got an action request to water the plants:

```
Event Published
Watering plants for 60 seconds
Event Published
Event Published
Watering plants for 60 seconds
Event Published
Event Published
Watering plants for 60 seconds
Event Published
Event Published
Watering plants for 60 seconds
Event Published
Watering plants for 60 seconds
```

At this point, you already have an IoT application and device connected and working properly in the IBM Cloud environment.

Summary

In this chapter, we developed a solution running on a real device that supports Node.js. We also used the low-level mraa library, which interacts with the device GPIO (General Purpose IO), reads analog sensors (temperature and soil moisture sensors) and uses digital pins to switch a relay on and off. This looks very simple but most devices have sensors and actuators, which may change the way in which they are used. However, they essentially follow the same concept.

We created a dashboard in the IBM Watson IoT Platform that is helpful for looking at what real-time data devices are publishing. We also created an application in the IBM Cloud Platform (Bluemix) and attached backing services (the IBM Watson IoT Platform organization) to the application in order to leverage configuration data to connect to the service and deploy the application using the Bluemix command-line interface.

The next chapters will introduce blockchain as a platform for interconnected businesses and explain its value and the common use cases in which it adds value to the business chain.

Further reading

Most of the resources needed to complete solutions using the IBM Watson IoT Platform can be found in the official documentation at the following link: `https://console.bluemix.net/docs/services/IoT/index.html#gettingstartedtemplate`. There are also many recipes published by the community that uses IBM Watson IoT, and these are available at the developerWorks Recipes website here: `https://developer.ibm.com/recipes/tutorials/category/internet-of-things-iot/`.

It's also very helpful to understand how to upload a project to a GitHub repository and how to create a delivery pipeline to automatically build, test, and deploy an application whenever a new change is pushed to the repository. Doing this is not within the scope of this book, but it's still a really good practice to use.

Further information on Grove system platforms, modules, bundles, and component specifications can be found on the manufacturer's website: `http://wiki.seeedstudio.com/Grove/`.

3
Explaining Blockchain Technology and Working with Hyperledger

Blockchain is a transforming force in a digital world in which people are connected more than ever. To explain it in a few words, this shared, distributed ledger known as blockchain is able to make the process of recording transactions and tracking assets in a business network more secure, easier, and with transparency for all members.

People now often use services such as internet banking, e-commerce, and apps for making purchases such as hotel reservations, taxi services, and other online services. This creates a huge volume of transactions and data. On top of this, IoT also brings new possibilities to this digital world. As products integrate with IoT, the volume of transactions grows exponentially; therefore, the necessity to connect to suppliers, banks, and regulators across geographical boundaries grows.

Blockchain technology provides a huge opportunity to transform operational business in many industries, such as financial services, insurance, communications, and government. Furthermore, it facilitates transactions between companies as they can be processed digitally.

What is blockchain?

Let's take a more in-depth look at what blockchain really is. An asset consists of anything that is capable of being owned or controlled to produce value. The assets are the protagonists of this network, and can include tangible assets such as cars, houses, or money. They can also include intangible assets such as copyrights and patents. If the assets are the protagonist, then the ledger is the *key*. The ledger is a business's system of records. Businesses will have multiple ledgers for multiple business networks in which they participate.

The following diagram represents the status quo for business networks. Each participant keeps their own ledger(s), which are updated to represent business transactions as they occur:

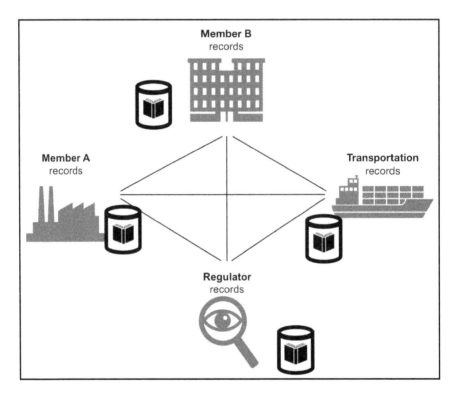

With blockchain technology, members of a business network share a ledger that is updated every time a transaction occurs through peer-to-peer replication, as depicted in the following diagram:

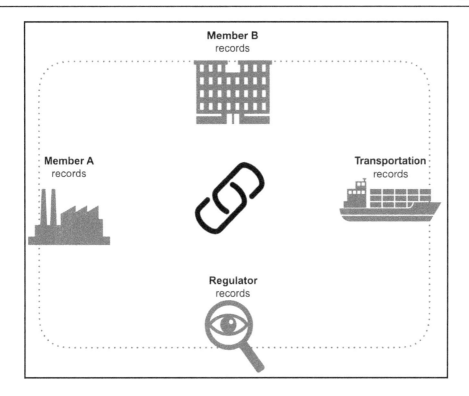

Blockchain allows multiple competing parties to securely interact with the same universal source of truth. It has shared immutable ledgers for recording transaction history, which provide a permissioned network with known identities.

The four important concepts of blockchain are as follows:

- **Consensus**: For a transaction to be valid, all participants must agree on its validity.
- **Provenance**: Participants know where the asset came from and how its ownership has changed over time.
- **Immutability**: No participant can tamper with a transaction after it has been recorded in the ledger. If a transaction was made in error, a new transaction must be used to reverse the error, and both transactions are then visible.
- **Finality:** A single shared ledger provides one place to go to determine the ownership of an asset or the completion of a transaction.

The main focus when we talk about blockchain is on a business network based on Blockchain, Blockchain for business, where transactions and members are permissioned, private, and prioritized; we are working with assets, identity, and selective endorsement.

You may be familiar with the idea that blockchain is a Bitcoin technology. In fact, we may even say that Bitcoin was the first use case of blockchain. Bitcoin is a digital currency with no central banks, no single administrator, and no paper currency. The software used is capable of solving mathematical puzzles in a peer-to-peer network. The transactions do not have an intermediary; they happen directly between users with transparency.

Blockchain and Hyperledger

There are many frameworks or technologies around blockchain: R3 (corda), Ethereum, Neo, and Nem, each one with a particular design and architecture. Throughout this book, we will focus on the blockchain technology Hyperledger (https://www.hyperledger.org/).

Hyperledger is part of the Linux Foundation, which was launched in 2016 with a technical and organizational governance structure and thirty founding corporate members. More than 230 members are now part of this initiative. This includes companies such as Cisco, Hitachi, IBM, ABN AMRO, ANZ Bank, Red Hat, VMware, and JP Morgan. Today, Hyperledger works with many projects under the same umbrella and focuses on differences in blockchain use cases, as well as covering frameworks and tools. A good description of Hyperledger projects can be found at https://www.hyperledger.org. Here, it is stated that Hyperledger incubates and promotes a range of business blockchain technologies, including distributed ledger frameworks, smart contract engines, client libraries, graphical interfaces, utility libraries, and sample applications. The Hyperledger umbrella strategy encourages the reuse of common building blocks and enables rapid innovation of DLT (distributed ledger technology)components:

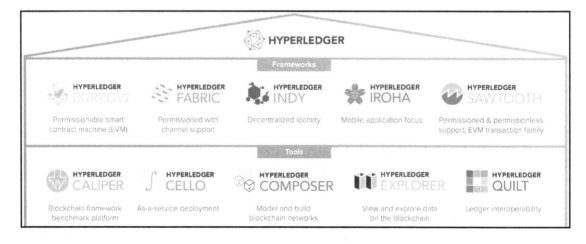

Hyperledger projects

Exploring the Hyperledger projects, we find five frameworks and five tools. The frameworks are Sawtooth, Iroha, Burrow, Indy, and Fabric. The tools are Caliper, Composer, Cello, Explorer, and Quilt.

Let's discuss these frameworks and tools.

Hyperledger Sawtooth framework

Hyperledger Sawtooth follows the same architecture and characteristics as other Hyperledger frameworks; it is an enterprise blockchain platform for building distributed ledger applications and networks.

In my opinion, the most striking characteristic of Sawtooth is the facility to use the APIs, as well as many languages such as Python, C++, Go, Java, JavaScript, and Rust. This aids in the development of applications that run on top of the Sawtooth platform. In addition, you can write smart contracts in Solidity for use with the Seth transaction family.

Another good feature is the parallel transaction execution. Most blockchains require serial transaction execution in order to guarantee consistent ordering at each node on the network. Ethereum contract compatibility can also be used with Seth; the Sawtooth-Ethereum integration project extends the interoperability of the Sawtooth platform to Ethereum.

Hyperledger Iroha framework

Hyperledger Iroha is a blockchain platform designed for building distributed ledgers; it is based on use cases such as Know Your Customer and features mobile application development and a new chain-base Byzantine fault tolerant consensus algorithm called Sumeragi. Soramitsu, Hitachi, NTT Data, and Colu initially contributed to Hyperledger Iroha.

Hyperledger Composer tool

If you want to test an idea, create a **proof of concept** (**POC**) or a minimum value product (MVP), or even start a project, then Hyperledger Composer can help you do so quickly and easily. You can test your business network with a web application named Composer Playground. With some clicks and a good use case, you can also create a business networking integrated into your systems. Another option is to create a frontend application to use your smart contract.

The picture below represent an official architecture overview in the site of Hyperledger Composer Tool.

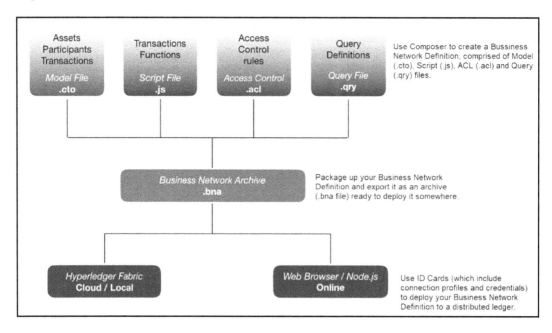

Hyperledger Burrow framework

The first paragraph of the Hyperledger Burrow documentation contains a good description of what this framework is. This description is as follows:

> *"Hyperledger Burrow is a permissioned Ethereum smart-contract blockchain node. It executes Ethereum EVM smart contract code (usually written in Solidity) on a permissioned virtual machine. Burrow provides transaction finality and high transaction throughput on a proof-of-stake Tendermint consensus engine."*

The idea is indeed to work with Ethereum smart contracts. The high level of architecture applied to Hyperledger Burrow can be seen in the following diagram:

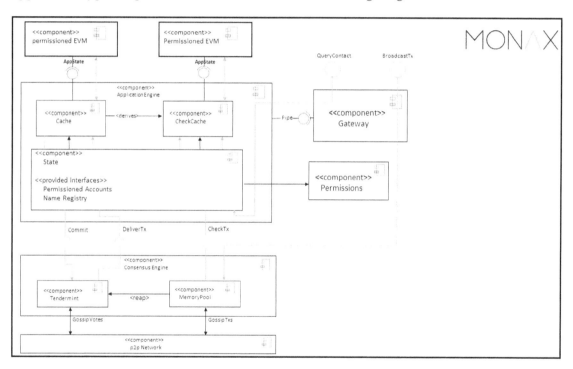

Hyperledger Fabric

To explore the umbrella project of Hyperledger, we'll work with Hyperledger Fabric. This was the first project or initial concept of the Hyperledger Framework, and Digital Asset and IBM were among the initial contributors. The characteristics of Hyperledger Fabric are as follows:

- Allows components such as consensus and membership services to be plug-and-play
- Leverages container technology to host smart contracts called chaincode, which comprise the application logic of the system

But before we move forward, let's review some concepts of blockchain and explore Hyperledger Fabric in detail:

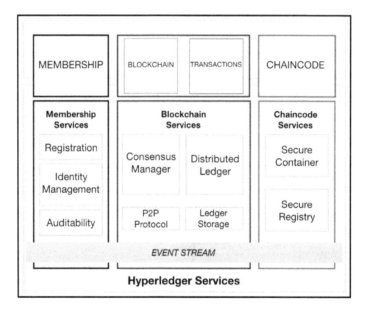

In the preceding diagram, you can see a high-level blockchain architecture. Let's explore (analyze) the important components of this architecture:

- **Chaincode:** This is our business network contract, and Just like a any contract, it states possible transactions between members of the network, and guarantee that every member has pre established defined access of the ledger
- **Ledger:** Think as a digital storage to entire transactions history, as a database you can have query capabilities to explore the data.

- **Privacy:** Channels: In the most of cases , there is an unique channel to all networks, but Hyperledger Fabric allows multi lateral transactions, guaranteeing the privacy and confidentiality, so if two members of the network for any reason need to have a specified transaction among them they can have a separated channel from the others.
- **Security and membership services**: Each member has a specific permission in the network , as a result every transactions will be logged and can be traced by an authorized regulator or auditor.

To explain what we are talking about better, let's take a look at the components of Hyperledger Fabric in a business network:

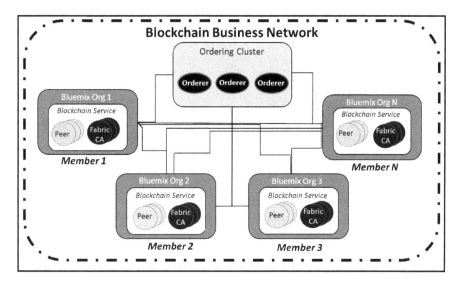

The components shown in the preceding diagram can be explained as follows:

- Multiple members are part of the blockchain network. In this case, we have **Member 1**, **Member 2, Member 3,** and **Member N**.
- Each member has its own peer.
- Each peer has a **Certificate Authority**.
- The queue or transactions will be ordered by the **Ordering Cluster**.

Member or peer

A peer is a member or a company in the network that hosts the ledger and smart contracts. Smart contracts and ledgers are used to encapsulate the shared processes and shared information in a network:

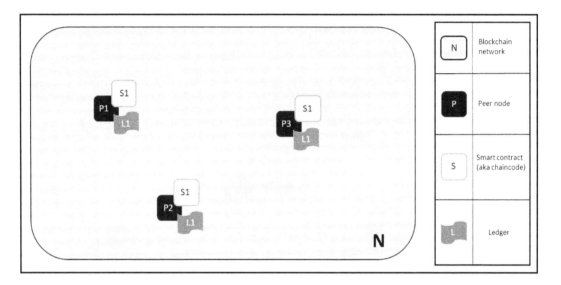

Certificate Authority (CA)

Each member of a business network can access a digital identity, issued for it by an authority trusted by the system. In the most common case, digital identities (or simply identities) take the form of cryptographically validated digital certificates that comply with the X.509 standard and are issued by a CA.

Ordering Cluster

The queue or transactions will be ordered by the ordering services that provide a shared communication channel to clients and peers, offering a broadcast service for messages containing transactions. As part of ordering and distributing the transactions, Hyperledger Fabric works with **ordering services (OS)** and a Kaftka cluster, which is the broker that guarantees the load balancing and consensus. We'll explore this in more detail when we set up the environment.

SDK/API

The application or current system can connect to the blockchain network through an SDK/API, which is normally developed using Node.js and is an important step in using the smart contract:

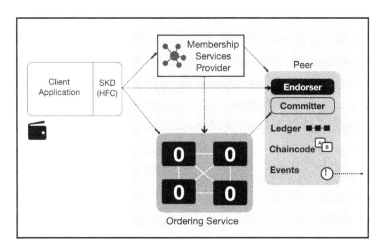

There are some important improvements in Hyperledger Fabric 1.3. Since version 1.1 and Node.js chaincode support, developers are now able to develop chaincode using the most popular framework with the latest programming language. If you are using a version before 1.1, you need to use Go to develop the chaincode. Let's explore the new features of Hyperledger Fabric 1.3.

The examples used to set up coding in this book will follow Hyperledger Fabric 1.4, with important new features such as:

- **New ways to develop applications**

  These new features facilitate the writing of decentralized code. They enable the developer to use Node.js SDK Node.js chaincode intuitively and logically to produce decentralized applications

- **New features for operations and easier to maintain**

  With more Hyperledger Fabric networks deployed and tested, serviceability and operational aspects become more important. Fabric v1.4 has new features for logging improvements, health checks, and operational metrics. Fabric 1.4 is the recommended version to start a production operation because its features focus on stability and some important fixes. If you go to the Hyperledger Fabric website, you can find information on future fixes that will be delivered in the v1.4.x stream, while new features are being developed in the v2.0 stream.

Selecting a good use case

Before we start any blockchain project, an important step is to select a good use case. We often see cases that can be solved through a distributed database or even a web application with good permission access. There is a puzzle to be cracked:

- Is a business network involved?
- Is there a transaction that needs validation or a consensus?
- Are audit trails important, or origin control?
- Immutability (data)
- Finality (fewer disputes)

Make sure to draw a map with different organizations on, or a business network and how they are connected—this is a very important step. Moreover, check the use case addresses one or more attributes listed between the second and fifth points. If you don't have more than one of the attributes listed between the second and fifth points, then it probably does not fit with the blockchain solution.

It's a good idea to have a think tank or design thinking session when selecting a use case.

This table demonstrates a good use case for different industries:

Financial Institutions	Insurance	Cross Industries and Others
• Credit letter • Credit debit or bond • Consortium shared ledger	• First party medical claims processing • Scheduled personal property claims processing	• Loyalty points • Capital asset management • Identity management

Blockchain – food tracking use case

Now, let's focus on the food tracking use case. Today, consumers are demanding more information and transparency on how and where their products are made. The EU requires more information about corporate supply chains, with huge penalties for companies and countries that do not comply. Since 2016, Chinese customers have been tracking where their food was produced, as well as how many times it has changed hands between different wholesalers and brokers before reaching their dinner tables. So, the use case sounds a good fit for blockchain, right?

Let's reflect on the five elements of blockchain:

1. Business networking

    Producers, manufactures, transportation companies, retail stores.

2. Is there a transaction that needs validation or consensus?

    Recording who owns what, when, and where an asset is in the supply chain.

3. Are audit trails important?

    Consumers request, blocks like E.U. and countries like China require a tracking audit.

4. Immutability and 5. Finality

    Different companies and assets involved in a complex process.

Okay, now that we know that blockchain fits with our use case, let's take a look at the benefits of using blockchain technology:

*   It is verifiable, preventing any party from altering or challenging the legitimacy of the information being exchanged.
*   Greater efficiencies are available through increased transparency in complex global supply chains.
*   Regulators, authorities, and business network companies can quickly and easily request reliable information from across the supply chain.

In the next chapters, we will be exploring in more detail the food chain, and how blockchain with IoT can transform it.

Summary

Blockchain features a shared and distributed ledger capable of making the process of recording transactions and tracking assets in a business network easier and more dynamic. This is different from Bitcoin, which is an example of an unpermissioned public ledger and defines an unregulated shadow currency with intensive resources. Blockchain is generally permissioned, private, and prioritizes endorsements, using assets based on a cryptocurrency.

The project known as Hyperledger is a collaborative effort with open source code that was created to promote blockchain technologies.

In May 2017, there were five active frameworks and five active tools:

- **Frameworks:** Hyperledger Burrow, Hyperledger Fabric, Hyperledger Iroha, Hyperledger Sawtooth, and Hyperledger Indy
- **Tools:** Hyperledger Cello, Hyperledger Composer, Hyperledger Explorer, Hyperledger Quilt, and Hyperledger Caliper

In the next chapters, we will explore in more detail how the blockchain platform can be used to solve some important challenges in the food chain, and we will discover that Hyperledger Fabric 1.4 is a strong blockchain platform.

Questions

Q. Why use blockchain?

A. Blockchain provides trust and transparency to solve food chain challenges that have stymied supply chains; with the use of blockchain, you can access the benefits of the platform, such as these:

- Trust and transparency
- Choose who is acting and receiving information, as you need only one shared ledger for transactions
- As the ledger is immutable, lack of confidence is no longer a problem, and participants can be sure of the origins and veracity of transactions
- Quick and easy access to detailed end-to-end supply chain data
- Minimize waste with better allocation of goods and products, based on data from the ecosystem

Blockchain gives participants the ability to share a ledger, which is updated through peer-to-peer replication every time a transaction occurs. Privacy services are used to ensure that participants see only the parts of the ledger that are relevant to them, and that transactions are secure, authenticated, and verifiable. Blockchain also allows the contract for asset transfers to be embedded, for execution with the transaction. Network participants agree how transactions are verified through a process referred to as consensus. Government oversight, compliance, and auditing can be part of the same network.

Further reading

To find further information about the topic, follow these links:

- The Hyperledger Sawtooth documentation, which can be found at the following link: `https://sawtooth.hyperledger.org/docs/core/releases/latest/introduction.html#distinctive-features-of-sawtooth`
- The Hyperledger Iroha documentation, which can be found at the following link: `https://www.hyperledger.org/projects/iroha/resources`
- The Hyperledger Indy documentation, which can be found at the following link: `https://github.com/hyperledger/indy-node/blob/stable/getting-started.md`
- The Hyperledger Composer documentation, which can be found at the following link: `https://hyperledger.github.io/composer/latest/introduction/introduction.html`
- The Hyperledger Framework 1.4 documentation, which can be found at the following link: `https://hyperledger-fabric.readthedocs.io/en/release-1.4/`

- GitHub Hyperledger Framework link: `https://github.com/hyperledger/fabric`

Creating Your Own Blockchain Network

4

In this chapter, we'll create a blockchain network using Hyperledger Composer. We'll explore a simple use case in which the asset can be transferred between the networking participants. We'll learn how to quickly install Hyperledger Fabric version 1.1. Also, we'll identify and implement a step-by-step guide for running your own business network.

We'll learn all of this by exploring the following topics:

- Pre-requisites for creating a blockchain network
- A brief overview of Hyperledger Composer
- Exploring the Composer Playground to create a blockchain network
- Setting up a local Hyperledger Fabric/Composer development environment

Prerequisites

To complete the exercises in this chapter, please ensure you have the following installed on your computer:

- curl
- Node.js 8.9.x
- Python 2.7
- Git 2.9.x or higher
- Go
- Windows 10/Ubuntu Linux 14.04/macOS 10.12

 For Windows 10, you'll need Windows Subsystem for Linux to run Ubuntu.

Creating your own blockchain network with Hyperledger Composer

In `Chapter 3`, *Explaining Blockchain Technology and Working with Hyperledger*, we looked at various frameworks that come under the umbrella of the Hyperledger distribution ledger. We then analyzed one of these, Hyperledger Composer, a powerful tool for developing a blockchain network.

In terms of blockchain, one of the biggest advantages of using Hyperledger Composer is the excellent documentation that comes with the framework, not just on the site itself, but also on the developer's website and other websites that hold examples of code and routines.

Here, we'll look at a step-by-step guide of a slightly less common use case than the one found on Hyperledger Composer's tutorial site, which will demonstrate how simple it's to create a blockchain network. We're going to use Hyperledger Composer's platform, which is called Playground.

Accessing Hyperledger Composer

The online Hyperledger Composer Playground enables us to explorer Hyperledger components without any installation. The following steps will guide you through a tour of the online Composer Playground:

1. Let's access the site at the following link: `http://composer-playground.mybluemix.net/login`. As we can see in the following screenshot, the home page opens with a splash page:

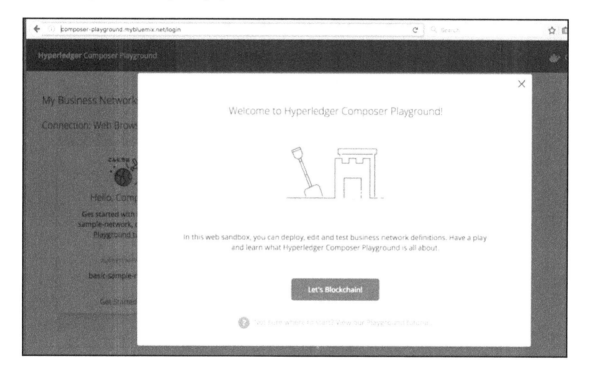

2. When you click the **Let's Blockchain!** button, you'll reach the next page, which works as a dashboard:

On this page, you have the option of using the tutorial, which takes you through a very detailed step-by-step process. This is great for exploring Hyperledger Composer. For now, let's move on.

3. Click on the **Get Started** link. After a few loading screens, you'll be taken to the editor, where you'll be able to create your own blockchain network:

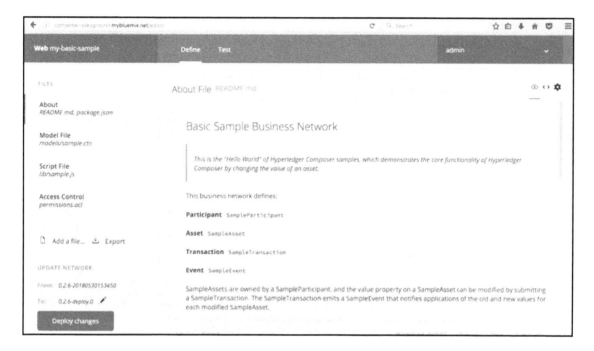

In our case, we'll have two participants and one asset, which can be a token that has a value. The idea will be to move this asset and the value between the participants of the network.

Exploring the structure of a sample blockchain network

1. Let's start with the `name.cto` model file. Model files define the assets, participants, transactions, and events in our business network. Remember that, after each step, you need to deploy the changes. Now we'll see some screenshots that will illustrate the process:

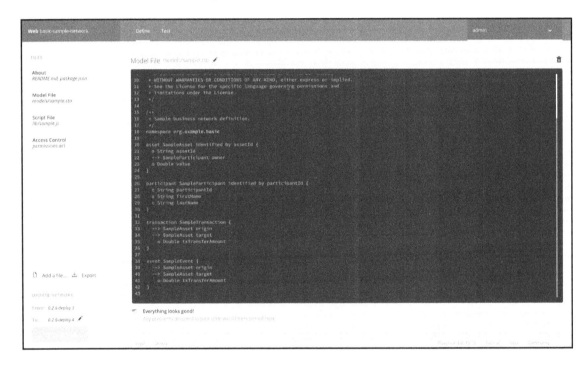

2. Let's use the following code to create the participants, transactions, and events:

```
// **
 * Sample business network definition.
 */
namespace org.example.basic

asset SampleAsset identified by assetId {
  o String assetId
  --> SampleParticipant owner
  o Double value
}
```

```
participant SampleParticipant identified by participantId {
  o String participantId
  o String firstName
  o String lastName
}

transaction SampleTransaction {
  --> SampleAsset origin
  --> SampleAsset target
    o Double txTransferAmount
}

event SampleEvent {
  --> SampleAsset origin
  --> SampleAsset target
    o Double txTransferAmount
}
```

3. Let's create a function to transfer the assets between the participants. We'll use the name.js script file:

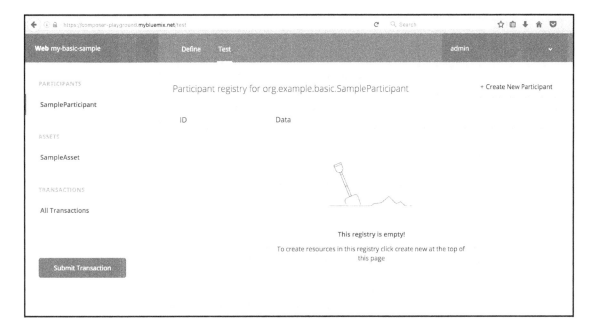

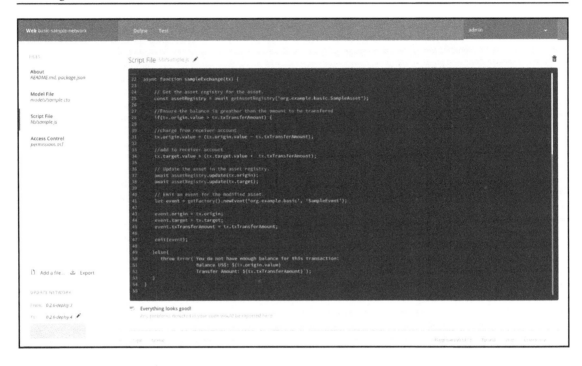

4. Let's look at the code that shows the algorithm/logic used here:

```
* Sample transaction processor function.
 * @param {org.example.basic.SampleTransaction} tx The sample
transaction instance.
 * @transaction
 */
async function sampleExchange(tx) {
    // Get the asset registry for the asset.
    const assetRegistry = await
getAssetRegistry('org.example.basic.SampleAsset');

    //Ensure the balance is greather than the amount to be
transfered
    if(tx.origin.value > tx.txTransferAmount) {

    //charge from receiver account
    tx.origin.value = (tx.origin.value - tx.txTransferAmount);
    //add to receiver account
    tx.target.value = (tx.target.value +  tx.txTransferAmount);
    // Update the asset in the asset registry.
    await assetRegistry.update(tx.origin);
    await assetRegistry.update(tx.target);
```

```
    // Emit an event for the modified asset.
    let event = getFactory().newEvent('org.example.basic',
'SampleEvent');
    event.origin = tx.origin;
event.target = tx.target;
event.txTransferAmount = tx.txTransferAmount;

emit(event);

} else {
  throw Error(`You do not have enough balance for this
transaction: Balance US$: ${tx.origin.value} Transfer Amount:
${tx.txTransferAmount}`);
  }
  }
```

5. The **Access Control List** (**ACL**) is the feature that ensures a Hyperledger Composer blockchain network segregates access for the actions that participants can take on the assets. Now we'll create a business rule to allow the members of the blockchain network to have the right access control. The basic file gives the current participant, the network admin, full access to the business network and system-level operations:

Here we have some code that shows us how to create an access control:

```
/**
 * Sample access control list. rule Everybody Can Read Everything
and send a transaction for example
 */
 rule EverybodyCanReadEverything {
     description: "Allow all participants read access to all
resources"
     participant: "org.example.basic.SampleParticipant"
     operation: READ
     resource: "org.example.basic.*"
     action: ALLOW
 }
 rule EverybodyCanSubmitTransactions {
     description: "Allow all participants to submit transactions"
     participant: "org.example.basic.SampleParticipant"
     operation: CREATE
     resource: "org.example.basic.SampleTransaction"
     action: ALLOW
 }
```

6. Define access to the access control's assets as follows:

```
rule OwnerHasFullAccessToTheirAssets {
description: "Allow all participants full access to their assets"
participant(p): "org.example.basic.SampleParticipant"
operation: ALL
resource(r): "org.example.basic.SampleAsset"
condition: (r.owner.getIdentifier() === p.getIdentifier())
action: ALLOW
}
```

7. Define a rule for `SystemACL`, whether network admin or user, as follows:

```
rule SystemACL {
description: "System ACL to permit all access"
participant: "org.hyperledger.composer.system.Participant"
operation: ALL
resource: "org.hyperledger.composer.system.**"
action: ALLOW
}
rule NetworkAdminUser {
description: "Grant business network administrators full access to
user resources"
participant: "org.hyperledger.composer.system.NetworkAdmin"
operation: ALL
resource: "**"
```

```
action: ALLOW
}
rule NetworkAdminSystem {
description: "Grant business network administrators full access to
system resources"
participant: "org.hyperledger.composer.system.NetworkAdmin"
operation: ALL
resource: "org.hyperledger.composer.system.**"
action: ALLOW
}
```

8. We're now ready to test our blockchain network. Click on the **Test** tab at the top of your screen:

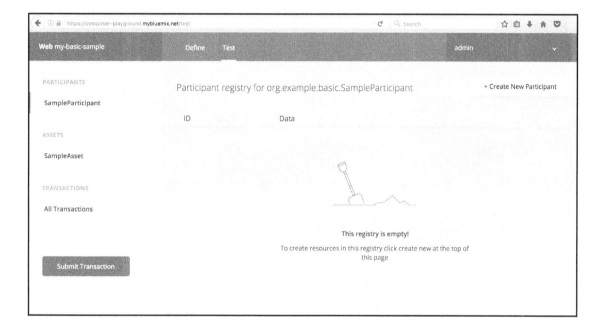

9. Now create two participants for your blockchain network. The first participant is shown here:

Use the following code to create the first participant:

```
{
    "$class": "org.example.basic.SampleParticipant",
    "participantId": "1",
    "firstName": "Joao",
    "lastName": "Dow"
}
```

The second participant is shown here:

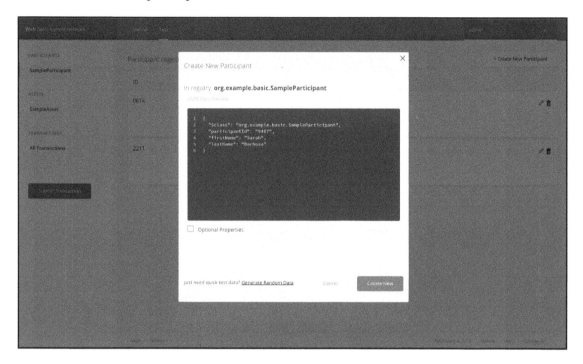

Use the following code to create the second participant:

```
{
    "$class": "org.example.basic.SampleParticipant",
    "participantId": "2",
    "firstName": "Sarah",
    "lastName": "Barbosa"
}
```

10. Now let's create an asset for participant 1. Remember to add `participantId`, `assetId`, and `value`:

11. Use the following code to create an asset for participant 1:

```
{
    "$class": "org.example.basic.SampleAsset",
    "assetId": "0744",
    "owner": "resource:org.example.basic.SampleParticipant#1",
    "value": 1000
}
```

12. Repeat the approach used for participant 1 with participant 2:

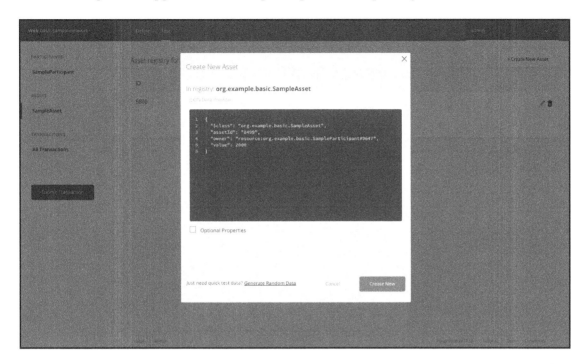

13. Use the following code to create an asset for participant 2:

```
{
    "$class": "org.example.basic.SampleAsset",
    "assetId": "4010",
    "owner": "resource:org.example.basic.SampleParticipant#2",
    "value": 1000
}
```

14. We're now ready to submit a transaction between the participants. Click on the **Submit** button and send an amount from participant 2 to participant 1. In the following example, the value of the transaction is **300**:

15. Use the following code to transfer an amount between the participants:

```
{
    "$class": "org.example.basic.SampleTransaction",
    "origin": "resource:org.example.basic.SampleAsset#0744",
    "target": "resource:org.example.basic.SampleAsset#4010",
    "txTransferAmount": 300
}
```

Great job! You can see all of the transaction details by clicking on the records in the two following screenshots. The first one shows a list of all created assets:

This second screenshot shows the history of transactions that have run on the blockchain network:

Now that you have validated a use case, you're ready to make a new proof of concept and present the full potential of the Hyperledger blockchain for members in the business network.

Installing your own blockchain network using Hyperledger Fabric and Composer

In the previous section, we saw how easy it's to work with Hyperledger Composer using Playground. Now we'll install Composer in your own (local) machine.

We'll start with the three most important stages of installing a blockchain network:

1. Installing the prerequisites
2. Installing Hyperledger Composer (the development environment)
3. Updating the environment

We can install the blockchain network using Hyperledger Fabric by many means, including local servers, Kubernetes, IBM Cloud, and Docker. To begin with, we'll explore Docker and Kubernetes.

Setting up Docker

Docker can be installed using information provided on `https://www.docker.com/get-started`.

Hyperledger Composer works with two versions of Docker:

- Docker Composer version 1.8 or higher
- Docker Engine version 17.03 or higher

If you already have Docker installed but you're not sure about the version, you can find out what the version is by using the following command in the terminal or command prompt:

```
docker –version
```

> Be careful: many Linux-based operating systems, such as Ubuntu, come with the most recent version of Python (Python 3.5.1). In this case, it's important to get Python version 2.7. You can get it here: `https://www.python.org/download/releases/2.7/`.

Installing Hyperledger Composer

We're now going to set up Hyperledger Composer and gain access to its development tools, which are mainly used to create business networks. We'll also set up Hyperledger Fabric, which can be used to run or deploy business networks locally. These business networks can be run on Hyperledger Fabric runtimes in some alternative places as well, for example, on a cloud platform.

> Make sure that you've not installed the tools and used them before. If you have, you'll them using this guide.

Components

To successfully install Hyperledger Composer, you'll need these components ready:

- CLI Tools
- Playground
- Hyperledger Fabric
- An IDE

Once these are set up, you can begin with the steps given here.

Step 1 – Setting up CLI Tools

CLI Tools, `composer-cli`, is a library with the most important operations, such as administrative, operational, and developmental tasks. We'll also install the following tools during this step:

- **Yeoman**: Frontend tool for generating applications
- **Library generator**: For generating application assets
- **REST server**: Utility for running a REST server (local)

Let's start our setup of CLI Tools:

1. Install CLI Tools:

   ```
   npm install -g composer-cli@0.20
   ```

2. Install the library generator:

   ```
   npm install -g generator-hyperledger-composer@0.20
   ```

3. Install the REST server:

   ```
   npm install -g composer-rest-server@0.20
   ```

   This will allow for integration with a local REST server to expose your business networks as RESTful APIs.

4. Install Yeoman:

   ```
   npm install -g yo
   ```

Don't use the `su` or `sudo` commands with `npm` to ensure that the current user has all permissions necessary to run the environment by itself.

Step 2 – Setting up Playground

Playground can give you a UI in your local machine if using your browser to run Playground. This will allow you to display your business networks, browse apps to test edit, and test your business networks.

Use the following command to install Playground:

```
npm install -g composer-playground@0.20
```

Now we can run Hyperledger Fabric.

Step 3 – Hyperledger Fabric

This step will allow you to run a Hyperledger Fabric runtime locally and deploy your business networks:

1. Choose a directory, such as `~/fabric-dev-servers`.
2. Now get the `.tar.gz` file, which contains the tools for installing Hyperledger Fabric:

   ```
   mkdir ~/fabric-dev-servers && cd ~/fabric-dev-servers

   curl -O
   https://raw.githubusercontent.com/hyperledger/composer-tools/master
   /packages/fabric-dev-servers/fabric-dev-servers.tar.gz
   tar -xvf fabric-dev-servers.tar.gz
   ```

   You've downloaded some scripts that will allow the installation of a local Hyperledger Fabric v1.2 runtime.

3. To download the actual environment Docker images, run the following commands in your user `home` directory:

   ```
   cd ~/fabric-dev-servers
   export FABRIC_VERSION=hlfv12
   ./downloadFabric.sh
   ```

Well done! Now you have everything required for a typical developer environment.

Step 4 – IDE

Hyperledger Composer allows you to work with many IDEs. Two well-known ones are Atom and VS Code, which both have good extensions for working with Hyperledger Composer.

Atom lets you use the `composer-atom` plugin (`https://github.com/hyperledger/composer-atom-plugin`) for syntax highlighting of the Hyperledger Composer Modeling Language. You can download this IDE at the following link: `https://atom.io/`. Also, you can download VS Code at the following link: `https://code.visualstudio.com/download`.

Installing Hyperledger Fabric 1.3 using Docker

There are many ways to download the Hyperledger Fabric platform; Docker is the most used method. You can use an official repository. If you're using Windows, you'll want to use the Docker Quickstart Terminal for the upcoming terminal commands.

If you're using Docker for Windows, follow these instructions:

1. Consult the Docker documentation for shared drives, which can be found at `https://docs.docker.com/docker-for-windows/#shared-drives`, and use a location under one of the shared drives.
2. Create a directory where the sample files will be cloned from the Hyperledger GitHub repository, and run the following commands:

```
$ git clone -b master
https://github.com/hyperledger/fabric-samples.git
```

3. To download and install Hyperledger Fabric on your local machine, you have to download the platform-specific binaries by running the following command:

```
$ curl -sSl https://goo.gl/6wtTN5 | bash -s 1.1.0
```

The complete installation guide can be found on the Hyperledger site: `https://hyperledger-fabric.readthedocs.io/en/release-1.3/install.html`.

Deploying Hyperledger Fabric 1.3 to a Kubernetes environment

This step is recommended for those of you who have the experience and skills to work with Kubernetes, a cloud environment, and networks and would like an in-depth exploration of Hyperledger Fabric 1.3.

Kubernetes is a container orchestration platform and is available on major cloud providers such as Amazon Web Services, Google Cloud Platform, IBM, and Azure. Marcelo Feitoza Parisi, one of IBM's brilliant cloud architects, has created and published a guide on GitHub on how to set up a Hyperledger Fabric production-level environment on Kubernetes.

The guide is available at `https://github.com/feitnomore/hyperledger-fabric-kubernetes`.

Our special thanks to Marcelo!

Summary

In this chapter, we explored an online cloud deployment of Hyperledger Composer through Composer Playground. By using the online network editor, we saw how to create definitions of the network, run tests on the network, and access the historian, where we were able to visualize all of the transactions that were run on the blockchain network.

We also ran the installation of a local development environment and gave you a resource to use to set up a production-level Hyperledger setup running on Kubernetes.

In the next chapter, we'll explore the main actors in the modern food chain and their current challenges. We'll then discuss how IoT and blockchain technology can help to solve these challenges.

Further reading

- For more information about Composer, visit `https://hyperledger.github.io/composer/latest/tutorials/tutorials`.
- If you want to install the full stack of Hyperledger Fabric, follow the recommendations at this link: `https://github.com/feitnomore/hyperledger-fabric-kubernetes`.
- All installation processes and architecture for Hyperledger can be found here: `https://github.com/feitnomore/hyperledger-fabric-kubernetes`.
- A step-by-step guide to installing Hyperledger Composer can be found here: `https://medium.com/kago/tutorial-to-install-hyperledger-composer-on-windows-88d973094b5c`.

5
Addressing Food Safety - Building around the Blockchain

In this chapter, we'll explore the main challenges of the food chain and understand the parties involved by reviewing the following:

- Current processes and problems
- The importance of product tracking
- Issues and concerns of governments and regulatory agencies

We will also see how IoT and blockchain are key technologies for addressing these concerns, as well as reviewing the certifications and regulations that are being put into place to ensure that the entire chain is compliant with food safety policies.

Regulations, challenges, and concerns in the modern food chain

Can you imagine acquiring a credit letter from a bank in a few hours, and sharing it with your providers in a few minutes? How about you receive an update from the customs department about the status of your goods with no bureaucracy and complete security?

Yes, this is all possible, and it is a fact that such information (product status updates, credit approval letters, and so on), gathered by using IoT and blockchain technologies, is important. However, the benefits brought by blockchain technologies go much further than the ones we've just mentioned.

Before exploring these additional benefits, let's go through some of the challenges that are faced by this industry and the regulations that are put in place to try and implement food safety.

Challenges regarding food safety

The CDC (Center for Disease Control and Prevention) estimates that each year 48 million people fall sick from a food-borne illness, 128,000 people get hospitalized, and 3,000 people die.

In a real-world case of a food safety concern, E. coli was discovered in spinach in the USA in 2006. As a result, spinach was pulled from every store across the country. It took two weeks to trace the source: 1 day's shipment of 1 lot from 1 supplier. In the meantime, there were at least 199 people who fell ill and 3 people died.

More recently, in March 2017, there was a huge scandal in Brazil involving the largest meat processing companies in the country. In an operation by Brazil's Federal Police called Carne Fraca, these companies were accused of tampering with the meat and selling it locally and outside the country. The corporations took weeks to respond to these accusations because of the difficulty accessing the data that was necessary to provide answers.

Food safety regulations – ISO 22000

As a result of globalization, many kinds of food come and go from different countries. There are a lot of serious consequences that can be brought about by unsafe food. This makes it necessary for there to be international standards to make sure that food is safe and that the food chain is in order.

ISO has a food safety management certification that can help to prevent such consequences. The purpose of ISO 22000 is to set down the requirements needed to make sure that all food is certified, and to guarantee that products are safe. It maps out what is needed from an organization, and it ensures that food meets requirements and is safe for consumers. It can be used by any type of organization, regardless of its position within the food chain or its size.

There are multiple reasons for improving the entire food chain. Despite several actions being taken to get better results in terms of higher standards of products, better storage, and higher production, little has been done in recent years to really solve these issues and be compliant with regulations such as ISO 22000.

The challenges are enormous in terms of achieving effectiveness in this complex chain, but we believe that the union of IoT and blockchain technology will mitigate many of these challenges and efficiently address the problems of this complex food chain.

How blockchain and IoT can help in a food chain

To achieve transparency across the ecosystem, we need to connect all entities that are part of it. This does not just pertain to retailers or manufacturers, but to everyone within the system; every member that composes it, from farm to fork, including the final member in this chain, the consumers.

Nowadays, there are a lot of companies in the process of adopting IoT and blockchain technologies. They have become aware that there are a variety of problems throughout the food chain, but each party focuses on their business results, not on the issues plaguing the entire chain.

Any solution that can solve this problem even partially will provide value to the entire food chain. However, it will still not solve every problem for all parties involved.

To implement an effective solution, let's review a set of needs based on market segmentation. Needs can change based on many aspects, such as company size, geography, and so on. Our goal here is to ensure that everyone sees the value of adopting IoT and blockchain technology and therefore becomes interested in participating in this kind of chain and its benefits. This will help us get the full set of data to provide end-to-end transparency across the food ecosystem.

Food ecosystem

In this section, we'll explore the participants involved in a food chain, and look at their activities and the regulations applied to each part of the process. We will look at the following participants in more detail:

- Farmers
- Food manufacturers
- Warehouses and distribution centers
- Transporters (transportation companies)
- Food retailers and supermarkets
- Consumers
- Regulatory agencies
- Certification and compliance

The following diagram shows all the actors in this complex food chain. The main purpose of this chapter is to identify how IoT and blockchain can be used together to increase the confidence in the veracity of information being shared, to reduce human error, and to ensure provenance with immutable data:

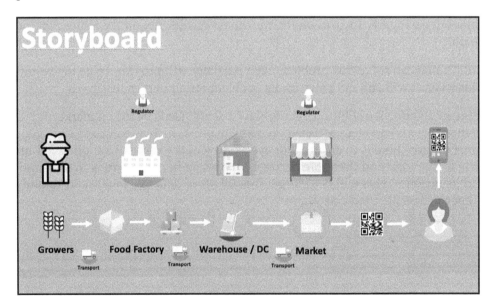

High-level food chain process

From a technological perspective, IoT is the icing on the solution's cake. Nowadays, there are a lot of asset-tracking sensors that can connect and transfer data via bluetooth, **ultra-wide band** (**UWB**), Wi-Fi, LPWA, LTE, NB-IoT, 5G, satellite, infrared, ultrasound, NFC, and RFID. This combination of multiple connections allows for asset tracking that provides instant information.

Now that you are able to access data by using IoT, think about storing this information in a blockchain network. Let's revisit the concept of the blockchain. First, we can say that a blockchain provides us with the trust needed for a reliable process, which was not previously present. But now, with blockchain technology, we are able to share many types of information across many ecosystems.

It also provides enough trust to allow us to truly solve the problems that we mentioned previously so that we can serve our customers in a better way. In addition to this, by creating this important trust, blockchain allows us to use the assets that we have already invested in. These are represented by the data that we've built up over decades and new types of analytics: cognitive, machine learning, predictive, big data, and many other similar ones. Moreover, we can say that blockchain represents the missing puzzle piece that brings these all together.

Some important things that our blockchain solutions need to achieve are as follows:

- Providing the transparency that the food industry needs
- Creating trustworthy connections so that everyone in the food ecosystem can participate
- Improving interoperability so that the industry can drive usability and access
- Monitoring livestock and grain monitoring
- Identifying the location of livestocks
- Greenhouse monitoring (temperature and irrigation)

Later in this chapter, we will look at how we can achieve all of this.

Opportunities and challenges in a food ecosystem

Let's explore each of the components of this ecosystem and identify the opportunities and challenges that come with them.

Farmers

Technology and agriculture work in concert and can be disruptive. Farmers are great at adopting new technology, especially when it helps productivity and delivers more efficiency in farming operations. These improvements are the motivation for adopting new technologies, and the reason is quite simple: the **FAO** (**Food and Agriculture Organization**) predicts that there will be 9.6 billion people on the planet by 2050, and food production will have to increase by 70 percent.

Agribusiness is the business of agricultural production. It focuses on the processing, warehousing, distribution, marketing, and retailing of products that are used in farming. Agribusiness popularized IoT solutions and put this technology on a different level.

Today, there are a lot of huge companies in this segment, such as Dow AgroSciences, DuPont, Monsanto, and Syngenta; AB Agri (part of Associated British Foods); ADM; John Deere; Ocean Spray; and Purina Farms. It is getting difficult to earn market share and make good deals in today's globalized world.

Farmers experience more pressure than ever to be productive. Therefore, they need to be concerned about topics such as the following:

- Keeping track of a production lot
- Creating a strategy for production warehousing
- Getting information about a commodity's market
- Identifying certain plagues in a faster way
- Guaranteeing a good environment, routine, and slaughterhouse for their animals so that all animals are well-cared for and well-prepared

These are the main challenges that farmers face. They rely on sensors; data collectors for measuring temperature, time, and the area to harvest; faster harvesting machines; GPS; predictive models supporting decision making; and blockchains to guarantee the storage of information in a precise and transparent way.

Food manufacturers

Food manufacturers play an important role in this chain; they are at the heart of this process. Because they are involved in everything from the beginning of the process (right from the early days of the animal's life) to the end (when the animal is slaughtered), they are also involved in the process of meat preparation and the packaging of consumer food products. Here's a glimpse into such a factory operation:

We have heard many times about constant problems related to food manufacturers, especially with animals such as chickens, cows, and pigs. These problems are often related to animal slaughtering operations, which have the highest number of incidents in the food manufacturing industry. Moreover, the food chain and the processes that take place inside of it need to go through several security gates, such as temperature analysis, visual approval, packaging machines, storage, and transportation.

Inside this complex market, no producer wants to have their products related to an incident that could give them a bad reputation. There are a lot of actors inside this chain that can directly influence a clients' perceptions. The challenges facing food manufacturers are as follows:

- The need to further automate the handling of food, reducing or removing human contact altogether, and ensuring high sanitation standards in the process
- Earning loyalty from suppliers and guaranteeing high quality levels
- Effectively controlling stock and the dispatch of goods
- Data about the location of storage and about where an action was taken
- How to register boxes, pallets, and the like

The industry has realized that IoT with blockchain technology can be a strong ally to guarantee transparency, traceability, quick resolutions for problems, and to reach a consensus, not just in internal departments but also with external partners and associates.

Regulators

For the food manufacturing sector of regulators, IoT and blockchain can provide more transparency in data, quick responses to data analysis, and other improvements, such as food origin certification:

In July 2018, the **Food Standards Agency** (**FSA**), an independent government department working across England, Wales, and Northern Ireland to protect public health and consumers' wider interests with regard to food, successfully completed a blockchain pilot.

Sian Thomas, Head of Information Management at the FSA, said the following:

> *"This is a really exciting development. We thought that blockchain technology might add real value to a part of the food industry, such as a slaughterhouse, whose work requires a lot of inspection and collation of results. Our approach has been to develop data standards with industry that will make theory reality and I'm delighted that we've been able to show that blockchain does indeed work in this part of the food industry. I think there are great opportunities now for industry and government to work together to expand and develop this approach."*

The government's role is to be the one that regulates. It is clear that other organizations that act in this area, alongside the government, now have trouble clearing inspections. Even though there are several control mechanisms, such as visual analysis and lab data that needs to be obtained by producers, inspections are still susceptible to corruption and do not have complete information regarding origin control.

However, as is obvious, the chain is long, and finding the actual responsible party for any deviation in a quick and objective way is not an easy task. In addition, the corruption that is always present in this kind of activity also affects the whole chain.

From this information, we can conclude that the following challenges in this link of the chain need to be addressed:

- Guaranteeing that the formulation of products follows the rules specified for those products
- Ensuring that information is reliable and auditable

Let's move on to the next link: transporters.

Transporters (transportation companies)

When we talk about food transportation, we should first talk about perishable products. Their handling requires special controls for temperature and delivery times, among other factors. There are also special licenses for transporting perishable goods. Special product inspections of goods at their destination and place of departure, and packing and unpacking, all need controlling and tracking.

Today, transportation companies have an arsenal of technologies that can help to address the control and tracking of products. Distribution centers and warehouses can control the arrival and dispatch of pallets with scanners, barcodes, and even by using robots.

Additional important facilitators are analytics solutions and the automation of invoices to track where an item was ordered from, supplied from, dispatched from, delivered to, and its arrival date. Image recognition, for example, can help register an item that has similar parts.

Without a doubt, IoT-powered sensors are a robust framework for these new technologies. These sensors can track temperature, humidity, and the tampering of containers for perishables and other goods. The devices issue auto-alerts to supply chain managers as soon as any given condition is violated so that food safety issues are immediately actionable.

It is at this point that blockchain technology can be of great help in tracking and registering products, and bringing trust and consensus between all parties with a single trackable shared ledger.

Stores and supermarkets

These actors in the chain are the first to get feedback when there is something wrong with a product. They (stores and supermarkets) are also often blamed for problems with merchandise, because they are sometimes responsible for storage, transportation, and product handling. These problems can happen inside a store or during distribution to other stores.

The operations performed at supermarkets and stores are as complex as the ones that are performed at food factories. They both have strong handling operations and responsibilities regarding storage. It is not unusual to have issues regarding spoiled food, and the question that arises is: *"Was this product already rotten or did it become rotten here?"*

Usually, each product owner has their own quality control process, and that make things a lot harder. When an incident occurs, parties provide evidence that absolves them of any blame, but that evidence is generally related to their internal processes. The process while transferring the product to another party is left unaddressed.

In addition, we have the distribution of products to bigger stores, where the same handling issues occur. However, these kinds of problems can happen at the store itself.

This gives us the current challenges that are faced by supermarkets:

- Managing and controlling the receipt and delivery of products
- Effectively controlling stock and the dispatch of goods between stores
- Collecting data about the product's physical location and storage
- Unpacking and transporting products to the shelves
- Controlling and being aware of product expiration dates

The majority of big and medium-sized supermarkets already have their own e-commerce networks. This results in the further adoption of technologies and software in their daily routines. As examples of technology used by these companies, we can mention stock control, the massive use of IoT to control boxes and pallets, the use of QR codes, integrated data systems to handle stock and sales, predictive models, tracking client loyalty, and so on. This shows us the increasing use of technology in this area.

Customer

In a competitive market, the customer is the protagonist. They will decide what the best product is out of the ones available on the market. Besides looking at the product itself, they will also decide the best place to buy the product and the best manufacturer.

Today, apart from providing great packaging, it is important for a store to have a perfect layout and to provide easy-to-read descriptions of products and items. Information about the origins of a product, whether it meets the standards required, and whether it has the necessary certifications is also of huge importance to customers. Some differential factors for customers when choosing their products are having easy access to all of this information, reading QR codes, and being able to listen to product details using an augmented reality solution.

Customers are more selective before buying a product that they will eat, have more opportunities to interact with products, and know more about how food impacts on their bodies, said a pair of futurists at a July U.S. Chamber of Commerce event. You can find out more about this here: https://www.fooddive.com/news/what-will-grocery-shopping-look-like-in-the-future/447503/.

The challenges within this chain are not easy to overcome. The possible impact of problems can result in much more than financial loss; they can lead to health issues for customers, or even death.

Technology can be a great ally to solve these issues. It's certain that, when we talk about IoT and blockchain, this combination can revolutionize this sector by bringing transparency between members in shared process chains, allowing them to control data more efficiently, increasing security, making processes automatic and dynamic, removing middlemen, and making the chain less complex.

We can also see that all of the members within the chain have huge challenges of their own and that the use of IoT and blockchain technologies can bring positive results. A better product position or brand equity for the customer can result in more power in their choices and an awareness of what they are consuming.

Is the food chain a good use case for IoT and blockchain technology?

Let's recall an important item that was mentioned in `Chapter 3`, *Explaining Blockchain Technology and Working with Hyperledger*. Here are a few questions that can be used to identify a good use case for blockchain:

1. Is there a business network?

    Yes—producers, manufactures, transportation companies, and retail stores.

2. Is there a transaction that needs validation or consensus?

    Yes—recording who owns what, and when and where an asset is in the supply chain.

3. Are audit trails important (showing provenance)?

    Yes—customer requests, regulatory agency requirements.

4. Is there any need to track data changes (data immutability and finality)?

    Yes—it involves different companies, and asset(s) are passed on from one party to another, which has different levels of control.

So, our food chain example meets all the pertinent requirements for being a suitable use case for blockchain. But how does IoT feature in this scenario?

In more ways than one. For example, smart farming based on IoT will enable growers and farmers to reduce unnecessary waste and enhance productivity, ranging from the quantity of fertilizer utilized to the number of journeys farm vehicles make for a harvest. Food contamination and its consequences can be prevented by detecting potential trouble before it happens.

IoT allows for such real-time monitoring; it not only checks historical data checks but also provides cost savings as sensors allow maintenance engineers to notice changes to equipment in near real-time.

Summary

We have seen how complex a food chain is. Many actors are involved with high interdependence. We also observed that the food industry has many challenges in its chain, which causes risks for customers when an issue is found in any part of the food manufacturing process.

Moreover, we are moving past the time where workers need to be physically present to monitor every piece of equipment through which our food passes. By using internet-enabled devices, maintenance engineers are empowered to have better visibility of what is happening with equipment, inventories, and people.

Blockchain technology can offer a trusted connection with shared value for all ecosystem participants, including end customers. IoT use in the food industry, with technology such as sensors, barcode readers, and QR codes, is at the heart of this solution, and IoT integrated with blockchain can not only mitigate a lot of issues but can transform the industry.

Internet-enabled sensors fastened onto equipment provide critical insights into maintenance and food safety issues, including real-time system-generated alerts and notifications. Maintenance engineers are able to access this real-time data from anywhere via a smartphone or tablet. The capabilities of an IoT system for food safety include providing real-time insights into the status of food processing equipment, sending automated alerts as soon as any problems arise, and providing the recommended next steps for troubleshooting and resolving a problem.

In the next chapter, we will link the challenges of the food chain with the technologies that can mitigate them.

Further reading

- CDC is one of the major operating components of the Department of Health and Human Services: `https://www.cdc.gov/`

- Scandal in Sao Paulo: `https://www.brasildefato.com.br/2018/05/10/as-gestoes-tucanas-e-o-roubo-da-merenda-escolar/` and `https://www.gazetadopovo.com.br/politica/republica/desvio-na-merenda-escolar-pf-desvenda-escandalo-de-r-16-bilhao-4zr4w5xhhy18ja0skldd83cmf`

6
Designing the Solution Architecture

In this chapter, we'll review the architecture of our IoT- and blockchain-based solution for the food logistics network, exploring the following topics:

- **The business side**: We'll review the business components and the main actors on the business side of things, as well as the processes that take place between production and the consumer.
- **The technology**: We'll present a diagram of the technological solutions that we'll be engineering.
- **Software**: We'll present a diagram detailing the solution at the software level, examining layers and integration.

We'll also review some concepts and architecture involved in our IoT- and blockchain-based solution in more detail.

The business of food

The modern food chain is very large and complex. There are numerous actors involved that influence the making of the product and its delivery, whether directly or indirectly.

We'll be looking at this modern food production process, learning about the challenges of the modern chain and proposing a new one based on blockchain and IoT:

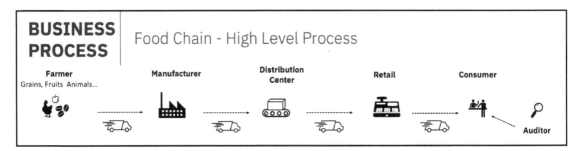

The business process shown in the preceding diagram is a simplified version of the modern food chain. The chain can be much bigger than the one represented here. For example, many supermarkets have their own distribution centers. However, since our main goal is simplification, we didn't represent other factors, such as ports and customs.

For our use case, we'll seek to account for the product from the time it's delivered to the manufacturer. This product could be any item, but we'll use chicken drumsticks for our example.

The asset to be managed in our chain will be a box full of chicken drumsticks, and our other asset will be a pallet full of boxes containing chicken drumsticks. In the food chain, we'll be looking at the processes of the following actors: the manufacturer, distribution center, and retailers.

As stated previously, there are a lot of actors in the modern food chain. Remember that we're following a more simplified process, not necessarily the actual process followed in real life. Our goal Here's understanding how IoT and blockchain can help the parties and processes inside the food chain.

Challenges of the process

The part of the food chain we have chosen to focus on has many challenges. We're listing them briefly here:

- **Challenges from the farmer's perspective**: Securing documentation of key information on raw materials, such as product descriptions, dates of inspections, date of abatement, and stock information

- **Challenges from the manufacturer's perspective**: Ensuring product origin and safe delivery and receipt of products, packaging products with electronics, using barcode/QR code informational labeling for regulators and consumers, and aggregating products into packages
- **Challenges from the retailer's perspective**: Checking package integrity and maintaining visibility of product packages across the transport lines with dates, warehouse validation, and quality control
- **Challenges from the consumer's perspective**: Having confidence in the origin of the product and the information contained in its packaging, as well as identifying goods quickly and, if necessary, removing suspect products from the shelves and consumption

The process at the food factory

Let's start from the beginning of our target process. In our use case, the product arrives at the factory in large pieces, where it'll be cut, packed, and put in boxes for sale. This product is stored and the boxes are put onto pallets before delivery.

A pallet is a wooden, metallic, or plastic platform used for moving goods, as we can see in the following diagram:

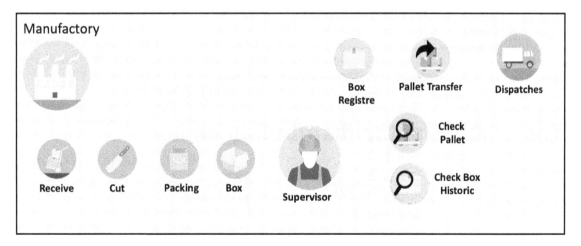

Next, we'll see the important data that must be registered about the product before it proceeds to the next stage. When the product arrives, the following data is captured and recorded:

- **Stock Keeping Unit (SKU)**
- Animal origin
- Name of producer
- Animal information
- Quality control
- Date of abatement
- Freezing
- Technical supervisor details
- Shipment date
- Temperature and transport details

The following details are captured during the registration of a box or pallet:

- SKU
- Date
- Factory address
- Freezing temperature
- Quality record
- Pallet code

Now let's check the process for the next actor in the chain.

The process at the distribution center

After being cut, packed, and delivered, the product arrives at the distribution center, where it's received and checked for storage. Depending on the process, it might go to a bigger pallet that suits it better for transportation, which could be by train or truck:

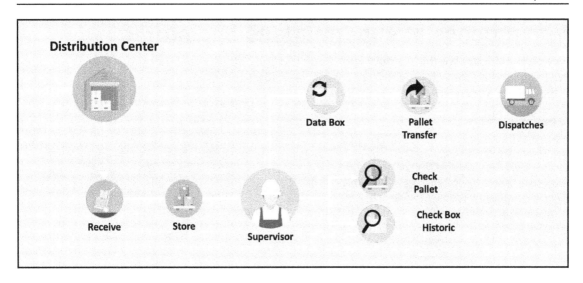

To avoid any issues with the product, the distribution center reviews the data sent by the factory. If there's any additional movement, such as pallet transfer, new information needs to be added to the package:

- For the product, it's the following:
    - Received date
    - Pallet number
    - Temperature received at
    - Temperature for storage
    - Transport company
    - Quality seal
- For the pallet, it's the following:
    - Destination code
    - Pallet code
    - Date
    - Temperature for dispatch
    - Transport company

After inspection, the products are sent to the retailers.

The process at supermarkets and stores

The store will receive the product and check the goods to see whether they fit the requirements. If they do, the pallets are disassembled and the boxes are opened. This concludes the monitoring of our assets:

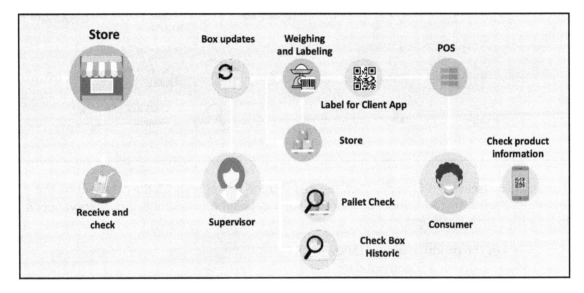

The following important data must be registered at this stage for the product to reach the consumer:

- Received date
- Pallet number
- Temperature received at
- Temperature for storage
- Transport company
- Quality seal

Now it's the store's responsibility to put a label on the product, after which, it may or may not be taken straight to the shelf.

The technological approach

Now that we have a better understanding of our process and potential problems, let's see how technology can be useful to us. Here's a representation of a standard blockchain Hyperledger Fabric architecture:

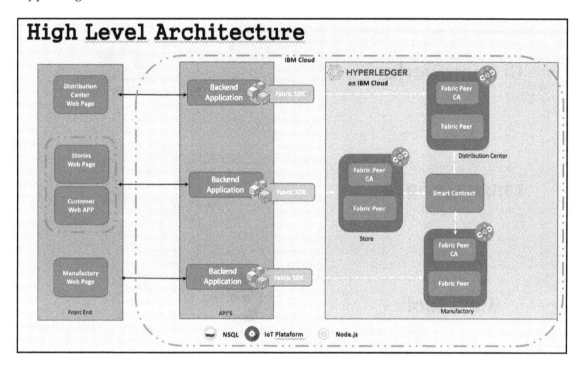

The preceding diagram shows us three important layers: frontend applications (on the left), API/SDK (in the center), and Hyperledger Fabric and the IoT platforms (on the right).

Let's review each layer in more detail.

Frontend applications

This layer is responsible for data input and can be a packet, such as one from SAP, Salesforce, or Siebel, or a custom application. It can also interact with IoT devices, collecting data and registering in the blockchain ledger. The modern architecture for developing frontend applications consists of these layers:

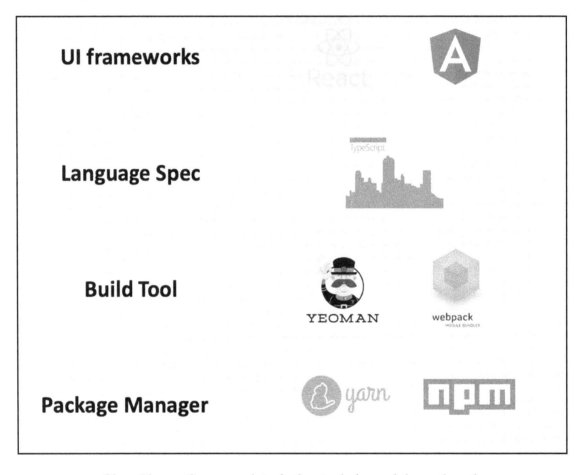

 Okay, I know there are a lot of other tools for each layer than those presented here, but I just used the ones I'm more familiar with.

This type of frontend architecture allows us to separate our services from a single interface. By doing so, we can expand the **User Experience** (**UX**) to several platforms without the need to rebuild the whole application.

IoT-based asset tracking

IoT plays an important role in the food chain. IoT devices can track assets, and there's an arsenal of models available that can do that. There are sensors for measuring temperature, and location can be determined using GPS, beacons, SigFox, Wi-Fi, 4G, and Sub1Ghz. These devices and networks can be used by farms, factories, transportation companies, distribution centers, and retail outlets, covering all actors in the food chain.

The major challenge in the food chain is transportation. Many foods require special care, and temperature is one of the most important concerns. Since many foods are perishable, and temperature control is vital for preventing contamination and damage.

Let's take a look at how we can mitigate this challenge using an IoT-enabled device. The Particle Electron Asset Tracker (pictured in the following diagram) can be used to collect temperature and environmental data and identify GPS location and cellular triangulation, among other things:

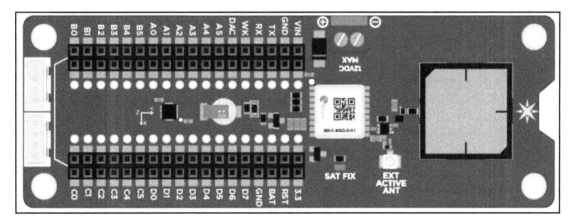

This tracker allows us to connect with a u-blox M8 GNSS GPS receiver and Adafruit LIS3DH Triple-Axis Accelerator. We can connect Grove sensors to it as well.

Let's look at a high-level architecture of this kind of IoT solution:

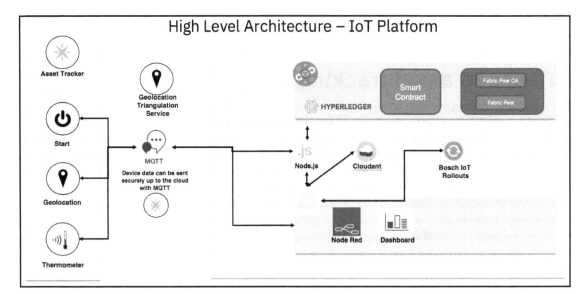

This diagram shows us some important components of the solution. Let's see what they are:

- **Message Queuing Telemetry Transport** (**MQTT**): This refers to a publish-subscribe-based messaging protocol that works over TCP. It's designed for connections with remote locations where a small code footprint is required or the network bandwidth is limited. The publish-subscribe messaging pattern requires a message broker.
- **Node-RED**: Node-RED is a programming tool for wiring together hardware devices, APIs, and online services in an easy way using a flow editor that can create JavaScript functions.
- **IBM Cloud**: This is a set of cloud computing services for business.
- **Bosch IoT Rollouts**: This is a cloud service in the Bosch IoT Suite that enables users to manage the rollout of software updates to edge devices, controllers, and gateways.

So, how do these components come together to assist in the various processes in the food chain? Here's how:

- The Node-RED control panel dashboard enables us to select an asset tracker and check the location, data, device status, and other information
- The asset tracker device can be either activated or updated over a cellular network

- Geolocation data can be transmitted periodically and can be followed by a dashboard in Node-RED, for example
- The asset tracker device queries the temperature data and then may query for location or velocity data
- Node-RED can write the temperature, location, and velocity data to Hyperledger Fabric
- The Node-RED dashboard queries Hyperledger Fabric for various tasks and information, such as transaction histories, date and time data, and geo-sensor data

API/SDK

The SDK or API is an integration layer responsible for connection in the blockchain network. It's normally developed using Node.js and plays an important role in the calling of smart contracts. Today, we can find API/SDK documentation covering Go and Java, with documentation for Python on the horizon.

 You can refer to this link for more information on how to use APIs/SDKs to integrate your application with a blockchain network: `https://hyperledger-fabric.readthedocs.io/en/release-1.3/fabric-sdks.html`.

The following diagram shows an application integrated with an API/SDK that interacts with Hyperledger Fabric:

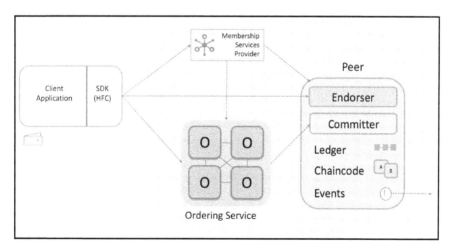

Composer JavaScript SDK is derived from Node.js, and it allows developers to integrate your application with their business networks.

There are two npm modules:

- `composer-client`: This module is usually installed as a local dependency of an application. It provides the API that's used by business applications to connect to a business network in order to access assets and participants and submit transactions. When in production, this is the only module that needs to be added as a direct dependency of the application.
- `composer-admin`: This module is usually installed as a local dependency of administrative applications. This API permits the creation and deployment of business network definitions.

Now let's move on to the last layer in our solution.

Hyperledger Composer – a high-level overview

Hyperledger Composer is an easy way to create your blockchain network, integrated with a full-stack working solution, as provided by the Hyperledger Composer architecture site.

At a high level, Hyperledger Composer is made up of the following components:

- Execution runtimes
- JavaScript SDK
- **Command Line Interface (CLI)**
- REST server
- LoopBack connector
- Playground web user interface
- Yeoman code generator
- VS Code and Atom editor plugins

It would be outside the scope of this book to review each of these in detail. You can visit this link to explore these components briefly: `https://hyperledger.github.io/composer/latest/introduction/solution-architecture`.

Software components

Now we'll look at the software components of our solution for an architect's perspective. This is a good way to get familiarized with all of the components and have a better understanding of how they are integrated.

To start, let's explore one of the most important components: the authentication process.

How we can guarantee that each member of the blockchain has the correct access permission in our frontend application? After answering this question, we'll delve into the most important components of Hyperledger Composer: the modeling language and the transaction processor functions.

Composer REST server

To authenticate clients, we'll need to set up a REST server. With this option available, the clients should be authenticated before they are permitted a call in the REST API.

The REST server uses an open source software named PASSPORT, an authentication middleware for Node.js. It's flexible and modular and supports authentication via username and password, Facebook, Twitter, Google, and **Lightweight Directory Access Protocol** (**LDAP**), among others. In Chapter 7, *Creating Your Blockchain and IoT Solution*, we'll have more details about this. For now, let's review how the components will work.

In the following diagram, we can see a high-level authentication architecture using a Composer REST server:

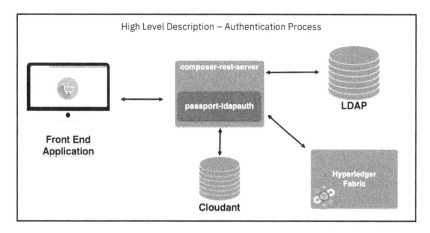

The following components have been described in the diagram: a frontend application, a composer REST server, LDAP, and Cloudant, a NoSQL database.

 If you're working on a test or need to create a proof of concept quickly, I strongly recommend using Facebook, Google, or Twitter for authentication. It'll be easier and faster than other methods.

To use the previous approach to use the composer REST server as custom implementation, we need to do some customization. Perform the following steps:

1. There's a following line the `composer-rest-server` installation that needs to be executed before the line:

   ```
   apk del make gcc g++ python git
   ```

   Make sure you have a clean environment before using this approach by cleaning all previous installations.

2. To customize our composer REST server Dockerfile, add the following command in the RUN statements:

   ```
   su -c "npm install -g passport-ldapauth" - composer && \
   ```

3. Create the following environment variables:

   ```
   export COMPOSER_CARD=admin@interbancario
   export COMPOSER_NAMESPACES=require
   export COMPOSER_AUTHENTICATION=true
   export COMPOSER_MULTIUSER=true
   ```

4. If you're checking the API call and receive 404, it means you're not logged on:

   ```
   export COMPOSER_PROVIDERS='{
       "ldap": {
       "provider": "ldap",
       "authScheme": "ldap",
       "module": "passport-ldapauth",
       "authPath": "/auth/ldap",
       "successRedirect": "<redirection URL. will be overwritten by
   the property 'json: true'>",
     "failureRedirect": "/?success=false",
     "session": true,
       "json": true,
       "LdapAttributeForLogin": "< CHANGE TO LOGIN ATTRIBUTE >",
       "LdapAttributeForUsername": "<CHANGE TO USERNAME ATTRIBUTE>",
   ```

```
    "server": {
    "url": "<URL DO LDAP>",
    "bindDN": "<DISTINGUISHED USER NAME FOR A SEARCH>",
    "bindCredentials": "<USER PASSWORD FOR A SEARCH>",
    "searchBase": "<PATH WITH USERS LIST WILL BE STORED>",
    "searchFilter": "(uid={{username}})"
  }
 }
}'
```

5. Check whether we have an API in our Wallet:

```
TestValideteLastProcess:A Transaction named TestValideteLastProcess
UpdateOpportunityStatus: A Transaction named
UpdateOpportunityStatus
Wallet:Business network cards for the authenticated user
```

To understand the process authentication better, let's explore this execution flow:

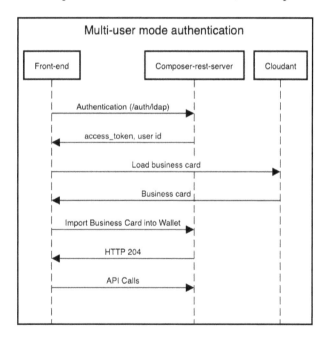

Each API call of `composer-rest-server` must include `access_token`, which is brought back by the authentication. For more information, see `https://hyperledger.github.io/composer/v0.16/integrating/enabling-rest-authentication`.

Some examples using `curl` are:

```
curl -v http://localhost:3000/api/system/ping?access_token=xxxxx
```

Here's another example:

```
curl -v -H 'X-Access-Token: xxxxx'
http://localhost:3000/api/system/ping
```

6. This is the final step in setting up your `composer-rest-server`: creating a business card with Cloudant.

Create member cards with the following attributes:

- **ID**: `wallet-data/admin@system name`
- **Key**: `wallet-data/admin@system name`
- **Value**: `{"rev" : "5-1af3gs53gwh...."}`

Upload the attachment as shown in the following screenshot:

In `Chapter 7`, *Creating Your Blockchain and IoT Solution*, we'll deploy this implementation.

Hyperledger Composer model

There are many ways to identify a blockchain use case. Let's remember some important indicators of a good use case described in Chapter 3, *Explaining Blockchain Technology and Working with Hyperledger*:

- Is there a business network involved?
- If yes, is there a transaction that needs validation and is auditable?
- Are transparency and data immutability important?

After determining the answers to these questions, brainstorm sessions are also a good way to detail the solution and identify the best solution platform (such as IBM Food Safety), or to start creating a custom development for the use case.

Using Hyperledger Composer Modeling Language can be an easy way to define the structure of the resource that'll be processed as a transaction and stored on the ledger.

The CTO file creates the domain model for a business network definition with three major elements:

- A single namespace that contains all resource declarations within the file
- A set of resource definitions encompassing assets, transactions, participants, and events
- Optional import declarations that import resources from other namespaces

In Chapter 7, *Creating Your Blockchain and IoT Solution*, we created a business network. Let's explore the code we used in more detail:

A namespace is the base definition of an asset, event, participant, and transaction, as you can see here:

```
// **
 * Sample business network definition.
 */
namespace org.example.basic
```

The declaration of resources and enumerated types is shown in the following code:

```
asset SampleAsset identified by assetId {
  o String assetId
  --> SampleParticipant owner
  o Double value
}

participant SampleParticipant identified by participantId {
```

```
    o String participantId
    o String firstName
    o String lastName
}
```

Transaction process functions are automatically invoked by the runtime when transactions are submitted using the Business Network Connection API:

```
transaction SampleTransaction {
   --> SampleAsset origin
   --> SampleAsset target
     o Double txTransferAmount
}

event SampleEvent {
   --> SampleAsset origin
   --> SampleAsset target
     o Double txTransferAmount
}
```

For more information about Hyperledger Composer Modeling Language, you can visit the following links:

- https://hyperledger.github.io/composer/v0.16/reference/cto_language. html
- https://hyperledger.github.io/composer/v0.16/reference/js_scripts.html

The Hyperledger Composer access control language

Hyperledger Composer has an access control file (.acl) with which you can program business access control and network access control. Business access control is for resources within a business network, whereas network access control refers to control over administrative network changes.

Here's an example of network access control being granted:

```
rule networkControlPermission {
  description:  "networkControl can access network commands"
  participant: "org.acme.foodchain.auction.networkControl"
  operation: READ, CREATE, UPDATE
  resource: "org.hyperledger.composer.system.Network"
  action: ALLOW
}
```

Here's another example:

```
rule SampleConditionalRuleWithTransaction {
    description: "Description of the ACL rule"
    participant(m): "org.foodchain..SampleParticipant"
    operation: ALL
    resource(v): "org.example.SampleAsset"
    transaction(tx): "org.example.SampleTransaction"
    condition: (v.owner.getIdentifier() == m.getIdentifier())
    action: ALLOW
}
```

You can get further information about the Hyperledger Composer access control language by accessing the following link: `https://hyperledger.github.io/composer/v0.16/reference/acl_language.html`.

Hyperledger Composer transaction processor functions

A Hyperledger Composer business network definition is composed of a set of model files and a set of scripts. The scripts may contain transaction processor functions that implement the transactions defined in the business network definition's model files.

Here's an example of a script file with a transaction:

```
Sample transaction processor function.
  * @param {org.example.basic.SampleTransaction} tx The sample transaction
instance.
  * @transaction
  */
 async function sampleExchange(tx) {
    // Get the asset registry for the asset.
    const assetRegistry = await
getAssetRegistry('org.example.basic.SampleAsset');

    //Ensure the balance is greather than the amount to be transfered
    if(tx.origin.value > tx.txTransferAmount) {

    //charge from receiver account
    tx.origin.value = (tx.origin.value - tx.txTransferAmount);
    //add to receiver account
    tx.target.value = (tx.target.value +  tx.txTransferAmount);
    // Update the asset in the asset registry.
    await assetRegistry.update(tx.origin);
    await assetRegistry.update(tx.target);
```

```
// Emit an event for the modified asset.
let event = getFactory().newEvent('org.example.basic', 'SampleEvent');
event.origin = tx.origin;
event.target = tx.target;
event.txTransferAmount = tx.txTransferAmount;

emit(event);

}else{
throw Error(`You do not have enough balance for this transaction:
Balance US$: ${tx.origin.value}
Transfer Amount: ${tx.txTransferAmount}`);
}
}
```

As we can see, transaction processor functions are automatically invoked by the runtime when transactions are submitted using the `BusinessNetworkConnection` API. Decorators within documentation comments are used to annotate the functions with the metadata required for runtime processing, and each transaction type has an associated registry for storing the transactions.

Summary

The architecture described in this chapter involves many components, and the implementation may seem a little complex. By now, we've established that the combination of IoT and blockchain can mitigate several issues and transform the workings of the modern food chain. For example, such an implementation can bring transparency between members, allowing them to control data more efficiently; increase their security; make the process automatic and dynamic; remove middlemen; and make the chain less complex overall.

We also saw that IoT works as the extension of computing and network capabilities for devices and sensors, enabling them to make machine-to-machine interactions with minimal or no human input. These technological components bring advantages such as unprecedented automation, cost reduction for provisioning, energy savings, value-added services, and efficient management.

Blockchain's integration with IoT will make possible data exchange between edge devices such as sensors, barcode and QR code scan events, and RFID-based assets. Assets connected with sensors will be able to record sensitive information, such as the location and temperature of a particular warehouse, and this information could be automatically logged or updated on a blockchain.

With a better understanding of the architecture and the elements that comprise its technical components, we'll be able to fully implement a solution with IoT and blockchain for the modern food chain.

In the next chapter, we'll see how to create our own blockchain with IoT.

Questions

Q. How can a lack of IoT security compromise data in a blockchain network?

A. Sometimes, companies don't focus on security when they work with IoT. Perhaps because it's a new technology, they don't believe it comes with imminent risk. The fact is, however, that businesses are bringing insecure devices into their networks and then failing to update the software. Not applying security patches isn't a new phenomenon, but insecure IoT devices with a connection to the internet is a disaster waiting to happen; think hackers and DDoS attacks. A strong security plan should be developed for IoT devices, similar to the one for internet services. Strong device identification and updates can help mitigate most problems.

Q. Is blockchain technology mature enough for this application?

A. Today, there're a number of blockchain platform providers available on the market. Carrefour, Walmart, and others are already members of these platforms. So, this indicates that big companies are already running their businesses on a blockchain platform, and that such a platform is suited to this kind of application.

Q. How complex is it to implement a solution using IoT and blockchain?

A. Most of the technologies described in this chapter are open source and are used by a huge number of companies. This shows that we're not talking about something that's that complicated, but something that can be used by most developers.

Q. How complex is it to have a solution that covers the entire food chain?

A. Yes, it's not an easy task. You can start by validating the use case; a good use case is essential. Also, check whether there's a business network involved; remember, IoT also plays an important role in tracking the assets, and you should have a security plan for asset tracking as well.

Q. Should I be concerned about using an open source tool such as Hyperledger Fabric or Composer?

A. Hyperledger is part of the Linux Foundation, which has more than 250 companies as members, including leaders in finance, banking, supply chain, manufacturing, and technology. For example, IBM, Cisco, American Express, Fujitsu, Intel, and JP Morgan all use technology by the Linux Foundation. In other words, these tools are safe to use provided you employ standard security measures on your devices.

Further reading

- A better description of Hyperledger Composer can be found on the Composer website: `https://hyperledger.github.io/composer/v0.19/introduction/solution-architecture`.
- The main focus in this chapter was Hyperledger Composer. If you want to explore the architecture of Hyperledger Fabric, you can find further information here: `https://hyperledger-fabric.readthedocs.io/en/release-1.3/arch-deep-dive.html`.
- Yeoman is an open source framework that creates your frontend structure. For further information, visit `https://yeoman.io/`.
- Passport is an authentication middleware for Node.js. For further information, go to `http://www.passportjs.org/`.
- You can have further information about the Hyperledger Composer access control language by accessing the following link: `https://hyperledger.github.io/composer/v0.16/reference/acl_language.html`.
- You can have further information about Hyperledger Composer Modeling Language by accessing the following links:
    - `https://hyperledger.github.io/composer/v0.16/reference/cto_language.html`
    - `https://hyperledger.github.io/composer/v0.16/reference/js_scripts.html`
- Information about composer-rest-server can be found at `https://hyperledger.github.io/composer/v0.16/integrating/enabling-rest-authentication`.

7
Creating Your Blockchain and IoT Solution

With a correct understanding of the project objectives that were presented in the previous chapter, it's time to get the solution to work. In this chapter, I will guide you through creating a blockchain network using Hyperledger Composer.

In this chapter, we will cover the following topics:

- Creating a blockchain network
- Defining assets, participants, transactions, and access control lists using Hyperledger Composer
- Publishing the network to a Hyperledger environment

We will also borrow code from `Chapter 2`, *Creating Your First IoT Solution*, to create a device that will monitor shipments and interact with the blockchain network.

Technical requirements

To access the complete code, you will have to install the Hyperledger Fabric/Composer environment on your machine, including prerequisites, and an IDE that's capable of developing Node.js applications (Visual Studio Code is recommended).

The code listed in this chapter is available at `https://github.com/PacktPublishing/Hands-On-IoT-Solutions-with-Blockchain/tree/master/ch7/hands-on-iot-blockchain`.

Solution overview

Here, we will be dealing with one of the most important parts of the farm-to-fork food life cycle: moving products from the food factory to the grocery store.

The following diagram shows the solutions that should be implemented for each of the given stages:

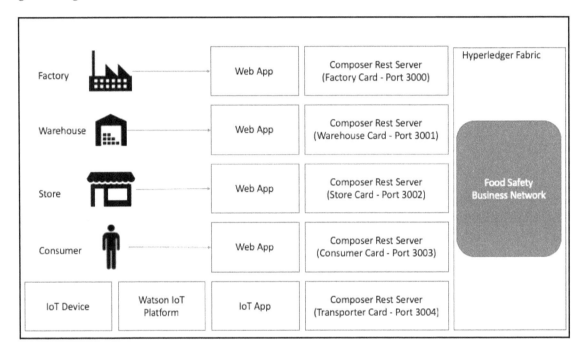

Let's look at the preceding diagram in detail. We will start with the four participants:

- **Factory**: This is the starting point of this food safety solution. It is responsible for gathering raw materials from farms and creating a box that is sent to the warehouse. The actions allowed for this participant are adding a new box and transferring the box to the transporter.
- **Transporter**: This is the company that's responsible for handling transportation from the factory to the warehouse and from the warehouse to the grocery store in controlled temperatures. The actions defined for the transporter are adding temperature measurements to an asset that is under its control and transferring assets to a warehouse or grocery store.

- **Grocery Store**: This is a company that sells the food box to the consumer. The grocery store is the end of the chain, and it's where the consumer can retrieve information from the food box. Grocery stores can check pallets and box data.
- **Consumer**: They are the target of the food box. The consumer is interested in tracking the box chain, so there's a mapped action of viewing the information for a box.

We will create an instance of the **Composer REST server** using a business card for each participant, and so we will have four **Composer REST server** instances in total. There's also the box and the pallet. The definitions for these assets are as follows:

- **FoodBox**: It represents the product that is produced at the factory and is handled throughout the entire chain
- **Pallet:** This represents a set of boxes that are grouped together to be sent from the warehouse to the grocery store

Let's start with our blockchain network solution.

Creating a blockchain network

To develop a blockchain network, we will first have to create a business network project using the Yeoman command line, and then name the business network:

```
$ yo hyperledger-composer
Welcome to the Hyperledger Composer project generator
? Please select the type of project: Business Network
You can run this generator using: 'yo hyperledger-composer:businessnetwork'
Welcome to the business network generator
? Business network name: food-safety-b10407
? Description: Hands-on IoT solutions with Blockchain
? Author name: Maximiliano and Enio
? Author email: max.santos@gmail.com
? License: Apache-2.0
? Namespace: com.packtpublishing.businessnetwork.foodsafety
? Do you want to generate an empty template network? Yes: generate an empty
template network
    create package.json
    create README.md
    create models/com.packtpublishing.businessnetwork.cto
    create permissions.acl
    create .eslintrc.yml
```

The Yeoman generator creates a folder with a basic empty structure for a Hyperledger Composer business network.

The `.cto` file contains the business network definitions: assets, participants, transactions, and queries, whereas the `.acl` file contains the access control list for the assets and transactions.

In later sections, we're going to code the business network definition, so start Visual Studio Code and open the folder that was created by Yeoman.

To start developing a blockchain solution, open the `models/com.packtpublishing.businessnetwork.cto` file and start coding.

Concepts and enumerations

It's a good practice to create combined data types that are common among assets, participants, and transactions by creating more readable structures in Hyperledger Composer. These structures are **concepts** and **enumerations**.

We will use the following structures in the solution:

```
// Tracking information when an asset arrives or leaves a location
enum LocationStatus {
 o ARRIVED
 o IN_TRANSIT
 o LEFT
}

// Location Types
enum LocationType {
 o FACTORY
 o WAREHOUSE
 o TRANSPORTER
 o STORE
}

// A measurement sent by the transporter sensor
concept Measurement {
 o DateTime date
 o Double value
}

// Check if it's in the factory, warehouse
concept Location {
 o DateTime date
```

```
 o LocationType location
 o String locationIdentifier
 o LocationStatus status
 }
```

Next, we will look at how to define assets in the business network.

Asset definitions

After defining the common structures of the blockchain network, let's define the assets that will be used in it. In our solution, we will have the `FoodBox` and `FoodBoxPallet` assets.

The following code defines them:

```
// Definition of a food box
asset FoodBox identified by foodBoxIdentifier {
 o String foodBoxIdentifier
 o Location[] assetTrackingInformation
 o Measurement[] measureTrackingInformation
 --> FoodSafetyParticipant  owner
}

// Definition of a pallet that groups food boxes
asset FoodBoxPallet identified by foodBoxPalletIdentifier {
 o String foodBoxPalletIdentifier
 --> FoodBox foodBoxInPallet
 o Location[] assetTrackingInformation
 o Measurement[] measureTrackingInformation
 --> FoodSafetyParticipant  owner
}
```

Participants

The participants are the actors that interact with the blockchain network. Each participant definition is for a different role in the business network and their permissions are defined in access control lists, as shown here:

```
abstract participant FoodSafetyParticipant identified by identifier {
 o String identifier
 o String name
}

participant FoodFactory extends FoodSafetyParticipant {
}
```

```
participant Warehouse extends FoodSafetyParticipant {
}

participant Transporter extends FoodSafetyParticipant {
}

participant Store extends FoodSafetyParticipant {
}

participant Consumer extends FoodSafetyParticipant {
}
```

Deploying and testing the business network for Hyperledger

For testing purposes, we will grant all participants full access to all of resources of the blockchain network:

1. To achieve this, we will add the following lines to the `permissions.acl` file (without deleting any existing rules):

```
rule Default {
    description: "Allow all participants access to all resources"
    participant: "ANY"
    operation: ALL
    resource: "com.packtpublishing.businessnetwork.foodsafety.**"
    action: ALLOW
}
```

With this rule defined, we will be able to deploy and test the ledger without any other extra permissions.

2. After defining the network, we will generate a **Business Network Archive** (.bna file) and deploy it to the Hyperledger environment. Make sure that your environment is up and running before that. To create the .bna file, go into the root directory for the project and run the following command:

```
$ composer archive create -t dir -n .
Creating Business Network Archive
Looking for package.json of Business Network Definition
    Input directory: /hands-on-iot-solutions-with-
blockchain/ch7/food-safety-b10407
Found:
        Description: Hands-on IoT solutions with Blockchain
```

```
        Name: food-safety-b10407
        Identifier: food-safety-b10407@0.0.1
   Written Business Network Definition Archive file to
        Output file: food-safety-b10407@0.0.1.bna
   Command succeeded
```

3. If you haven't generated the `PeerAdminCard` yet, it's time to do so and import it
   with the `createPeerAdminCard.sh` script inside the directory where we have
   downloaded the `fabric-dev servers`:

```
$ ~/fabric-dev-servers/createPeerAdminCard.sh
Development only script for Hyperledger Fabric control
Running 'createPeerAdminCard.sh'
FABRIC_VERSION is unset, assuming hlfv12
FABRIC_START_TIMEOUT is unset, assuming 15 (seconds)
Using composer-cli at v0.20.4
Successfully created business network card file to
    Output file: /tmp/PeerAdmin@hlfv1.card
Command succeeded
Successfully imported business network card
    Card file: /tmp/PeerAdmin@hlfv1.card
    Card name: PeerAdmin@hlfv1
Command succeeded
The following Business Network Cards are available:
Connection Profile: hlfv1
```

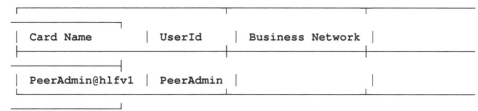

```
Issue composer card list --card <Card Name> to get details a
specific card
Command succeeded
Hyperledger Composer PeerAdmin card has been imported, host of
fabric specified as 'localhost'
```

4. When you have everything set up, install the `.bna` file into the environment and
   start the network by running the following commands:

```
$ composer network install --card PeerAdmin@hlfv1 --archiveFile
food-safety-b10407\@0.0.1.bna
√ Installing business network. This may take a minute...
Successfully installed business network food-safety-b10407, version
0.0.1
```

```
Command succeeded
$ composer network start --networkName food-safety-b10407 --
networkVersion 0.0.1 --networkAdmin admin --
networkAdminEnrollSecret adminpw --card PeerAdmin@hlfv1 --file
networkadmin.card
Starting business network food-safety-b10407 at version 0.0.1

Processing these Network Admins:
userName: admin
√ Starting business network definition. This may take a minute...
Successfully created business network card:
Filename: networkadmin.card

Command succeeded
```

5. Finally, import the network administrator card that was generated by the start process and ping the network to ensure it's running in the environment:

```
$ composer card import --file networkadmin.card
Successfully imported business network card
    Card file: networkadmin.card
    Card name: admin@food-safety-b10407

Command succeeded

$ composer network ping --card admin@food-safety-b10407
The connection to the network was successfully tested: food-safety-
b10407
    Business network version: 0.0.1
    Composer runtime version: 0.20.4
    participant: org.hyperledger.composer.system.NetworkAdmin#admin
    identity:
org.hyperledger.composer.system.Identity#f48a787ac40102cc7753336f8b
15dd20fa3765e7b9049b2aeda4dcc3816d30c1

Command succeeded
```

At this point, we have created the first version of our network; generated the package for deployment (the .bna file); created the PeerAdminCard; installed the network to the Hyperledger Fabric environment; generated the NetworkAdminCard, which is responsible for managing the blockchain network; and started the network.

With the Admin cards, we will send a ping command to ensure that the network is up and running. Now, let's improve our network.

Manipulating assets via transactions in the blockchain

Transactions are atomic operations that are performed on objects inside a Hyperledger Composer-defined business network. They run on the scope of the Hyperledger Fabric environment and the defined business network.

In the use case that's demonstrated here, the transaction that we've created will update both the pallet and the nested food boxes with the information provided by the IoT device.

It is composed of two structures. The first one is the definition of the transaction and is created in the business network definition model (the `.cto` file):

```
transaction updateTransportationData {
  --> FoodBoxPallet pallet
  o Location locationInformation
  o Measurement measurementInformation
}
```

The next structure is the function that implements the transaction that was defined previously and is created in a JavaScript ES5 compliant script (a `.js` file):

```
/**
 * Update pallets and boxes with measurements function.
 * @param
{com.packtpublishing.businessnetwork.foodsafety.UpdateTransportationData}
tx Update pallets and boxes with measurements.
 * @transaction
 */
async function updateTransportationData(tx) {

  // Get transaction parametes
  let newValue = tx.asset;
  let location = tx.locationInformation;
  let measurement = tx.measurementInformation;

  // Update Pallet data with measurements
  if( !newValue.assetTrackingInformation ||
newValue.assetTrackingInformation == undefined)
  newValue.assetTrackingInformation = [];
  if ( !newValue.measureTrackingInformation ||
newValue.measureTrackingInformation == undefined)
  newValue.measureTrackingInformation = [];

  newValue.assetTrackingInformation.push(location);
  newValue.measureTrackingInformation.push(measurement);
```

```
// Update Boxes data with measurements
let foodBox = newValue.foodBoxInPallet;
if( !foodBox.assetTrackingInformation || foodBox.assetTrackingInformation
== undefined)
foodBox.assetTrackingInformation = [];

if ( ! foodBox.measureTrackingInformation ||
foodBox.measureTrackingInformation == undefined)
foodBox.measureTrackingInformation = [];

foodBox.assetTrackingInformation.push(location);
foodBox.measureTrackingInformation.push(measurement);

// Get the asset registry for both assets.
let assetRegistryFoodBoxPallet = await
getAssetRegistry('com.packtpublishing.businessnetwork.foodsafety.FoodBoxPal
let');
let assetRegistryFoodBox = await
getAssetRegistry('com.packtpublishing.businessnetwork.foodsafety.FoodBox');

// Update the assets in the asset registry.
await assetRegistryFoodBoxPallet.update(newValue);
await assetRegistryFoodBox.update(foodBox);
}
```

Generating and exporting participant business cards

To use the network properly, we will create one participant for each class (`Factory`, `Warehouse`, `Transporter`, `Store`, and `Consumer`), generate their respective business cards, and import them into a Composer CLI Wallet:

1. First, we will create the participants:

    ```
    $ composer participant add -c admin@food-safety-b10407 -d
    '{"$class":"com.packtpublishing.businessnetwork.foodsafety.Consumer
    ","identifier":"5","name":"Consumer"}'
    Participant was added to participant registry.

    Command succeeded

    $ composer participant add -c admin@food-safety-b10407 -d
    '{"$class":"com.packtpublishing.businessnetwork.foodsafety.Store","
    identifier":"4","name":"Store"}'
    Participant was added to participant registry.
    ```

```
Command succeeded

$ composer participant add -c admin@food-safety-b10407 -d
'{"$class":"com.packtpublishing.businessnetwork.foodsafety.Transpor
ter","identifier":"2","name":"Transporter"}'
Participant was added to participant registry.

Command succeeded

$ composer participant add -c admin@food-safety-b10407 -d
'{"$class":"com.packtpublishing.businessnetwork.foodsafety.Warehous
e","identifier":"3","name":"Warehouse"}'
Participant was added to participant registry.

Command succeeded

$ composer participant add -c admin@food-safety-b10407 -d
'{"$class":"com.packtpublishing.businessnetwork.foodsafety.FoodFact
ory","identifier":"1","name":"Factory"}'
Participant was added to participant registry.
Command succeeded
```

2. Then, we will issue an identity and import their respective business cards with the following command:

```
composer identity issue -c admin@food-safety-b10407 -f <name of the output
file for the card> -u <participant name> -a <participant class# Participant
id>
```

3. Repeat this command for each participant: Transporter 1, Store 1, Warehouse 1, and Factory 1.

```
$ composer identity issue -c admin@food-safety-b10407 -f
consumer.card -u "Consumer" -a
"resource:com.packtpublishing.businessnetwork.foodsafety.Consumer#1
"
Issue identity and create Network Card for: Consumer

√ Issuing identity. This may take a few seconds...

Successfully created business network card file to
    Output file: consumer.card

Command succeeded
```

4. Import each card into the Composer CLI wallet for each participant/card generated and check that all cards have been imported successfully:

```
$ composer card import -f consumer.card
Successfully imported business network card
    Card file: consumer.card
    Card name: Consumer 1@food-safety-b10407

Command succeeded

$ composer card list
The following Business Network Cards are available:
Connection Profile: hlfv1
```

Card Name	UserId	Business Network
Factory 1@food-safety-b10407	Factory	food-safety-b10407
Warehouse 1@food-safety-b10407	Warehouse	food-safety-b10407
Store 1@food-safety-b10407	Store	food-safety-b10407
Consumer 1@food-safety-b10407	Consumer	food-safety-b10407
Transporter 1@food-safety-b10407	Transporter	food-safety-b10407
admin@food-safety-b10407	admin	food-safety-b10407
PeerAdmin@hlfv1	PeerAdmin	

```
Issue composer card list --card <Card Name> to get details a
specific card

Command succeeded
```

Defining access control lists (ACLs)

To enforce permissions on the network, we will define some access control for participants over assets with the following rules:

1. Only factories can create `FoodBoxes`:

```
rule FoodBoxFactoryCreation {
  description: "Factories can create FoodBoxes"
  participant:
"com.packtpublishing.businessnetwork.foodsafety.FoodFactory"
  operation: CREATE
  resource: "com.packtpublishing.businessnetwork.foodsafety.FoodBox"
  action: ALLOW
}
```

2. Since a food factory can also see what their `FoodBoxes` are and transfer them to a transporter, we can use a conditional rule to define these restrictions:

```
rule FoodBoxFactoryUpdateAndRead {
  description: "Factories can update and read owned FoodBoxes"
  participant(p):
"com.packtpublishing.businessnetwork.foodsafety.FoodFactory"
  operation: UPDATE, READ
  resource(b):
"com.packtpublishing.businessnetwork.foodsafety.FoodBox"
  condition: (p == b.owner)
  action: ALLOW
}
```

3. The next rule refers to `Transporters`. These can read and update their own `FoodBoxes`. We will do the same thing for `FoodBoxPallets`:

```
rule FoodBoxTransportersUpdateAndRead {
  description: "Transporters can update and read owned FoodBoxes"
  participant(p):
"com.packtpublishing.businessnetwork.foodsafety.Transporter"
  operation: UPDATE, READ
  resource(b):
```

```
"com.packtpublishing.businessnetwork.foodsafety.FoodBox"
condition: (p  == b.owner )
action: ALLOW
}

rule FoodBoxPalletTransportersUpdateAndRead {
 description: "ransporters can update and read owned FoodBoxes"
 participant(p):
"com.packtpublishing.businessnetwork.foodsafety.Transporter"
 operation: UPDATE, READ
 resource(b):
"com.packtpublishing.businessnetwork.foodsafety.FoodBoxPallet"
 condition: (p  == b.owner )
 action: ALLOW
}
```

4. Warehouses can also read and update their `FoodBoxes`, as well as creating, updating, and reading `FoodBoxPallets`:

```
rule FoodBoxPalletWarehouseCreate {
 description: "Warehouses can create FoodBoxPallets"
 participant:
"com.packtpublishing.businessnetwork.foodsafety.Warehouse"
 operation: CREATE
 resource:
"com.packtpublishing.businessnetwork.foodsafety.FoodBoxPallet"
 action: ALLOW
}

rule FoodBoxWarehouseUpdateAndRead {
 description: "Warehouses can update and read owned FoodBoxes"
 participant(p):
"com.packtpublishing.businessnetwork.foodsafety.Warehouse"
 operation: UPDATE, READ
 resource(b):
"com.packtpublishing.businessnetwork.foodsafety.FoodBox"
 condition: (p == b.owner )
 action: ALLOW
}

rule FoodBoxPalletWarehouseUpdateAndRead {
 description: "Warehouses can update and read owned FoodBoxes"
 participant(p):
"com.packtpublishing.businessnetwork.foodsafety.Warehouse"
 operation: UPDATE, READ
 resource(b):
"com.packtpublishing.businessnetwork.foodsafety.FoodBoxPallet"
```

```
    condition: (p  == b.owner)
    action: ALLOW
}
```

5. Finally, stores can read the `FoodBoxes` they own, while consumers can read all `FoodBoxes`:

```
// Store Rules
rule StoreCanReadFoodBoxes {
  description: "Stores can update and read owned FoodBoxes"
  participant(p):
"com.packtpublishing.businessnetwork.foodsafety.Store"
  operation: READ
  resource(b):
"com.packtpublishing.businessnetwork.foodsafety.FoodBoxPallet"
  condition: (p  == b.owner )
  action: ALLOW
}

// Consumer Rules
rule ConsumersCanReadFoodBoxes {
  description: "Factories can update and read owned FoodBoxes"
  participant:
"com.packtpublishing.businessnetwork.foodsafety.Consumer"
  operation: READ
  resource: "com.packtpublishing.businessnetwork.foodsafety.FoodBox"
  action: ALLOW
}
```

After applying these rules, the network is ready to be tested.

Upgrading the business network to a newer version

There are only four steps that are necessary to upgrade a deployed business network:

1. Open the `package.json` file and update the version number for the application. In our case, it will update to `0.0.2` and will look like this:

```
{
  "engines": {
  "composer": "^0.20.4"
  },
  "name": "food-safety-b10407",
```

```
    "version": "0.0.2",
    ...
```

2. Create a new BNA file by running the `composer archive create -t dir -n .` command:

```
$ composer archive create -t dir -n .
Creating Business Network Archive

Looking for package.json of Business Network Definition
 Input directory: /projects/hands-on-iot-solutions-with-
blockchain/ch7/food-safety-b10407
Found:
 Description: Hands-on IoT solutions with Blockchain
 Name: food-safety-b10407
 Identifier: food-safety-b10407@0.0.2
Written Business Network Definition Archive file to
 Output file: food-safety-b10407@0.0.2.bna

Command succeeded
```

3. Install the new archive file in the Hyperledger environment:

```
$ composer network install --card PeerAdmin@hlfv1 --archiveFile
food-safety-b10407\@0.0.2.bna
√ Installing business network. This may take a minute...
Successfully installed business network food-safety-b10407, version
0.0.2

Command succeeded
```

4. Finally, `upgrade` the network version to the new one:

```
$ composer network upgrade --card PeerAdmin@hlfv1 --networkName
food-safety-b10407 --networkVersion 0.0.2
Upgrading business network food-safety-b10407 to version 0.0.2

√ Upgrading business network definition. This may take a minute...

Command succeeded
```

If all of the commands have run successfully, the business network will now be running on the new version, including the transactions and ACLs that were created in the preceding sections.

Setting up Composer REST servers for each participant

As part of the prerequisites for the installation of the Hyperledger Composer development environment, you would have also installed the Composer REST server.

This component is an API server based on the Loopback framework (`http://loopback.io`) and includes a `loopback-connector-composer` to connect to the Hyperledger Composer environment and a script that dynamically gather assets, participants, and transactions models.

The easiest way of starting a Composer REST server is by running the `cli` commands and filling the startup questionnaire correctly. For our convenience, we will be running it using the following command:

```
composer-rest-server -c "<business card name>" -n never -u true -w true -p
<port defined for the participant server>
```

Open a terminal window for each participant to start a dedicated Composer REST server for it:

```
composer-rest-server -c "Factory@food-safety-b10407" -n never -u true -w
true -p 3000

composer-rest-server -c "Warehouse@food-safety-b10407" -n never -u true -w
true -p 3001

composer-rest-server -c "Store@food-safety-b10407" -n never -u true -w true
-p 3002

composer-rest-server -c "Consumer@food-safety-b10407" -n never -u true -w
true -p 3003

composer-rest-server -c "Transporter@food-safety-b10407" -n never -u true -
w true -p 3004
```

Each running instance is related to a single user, meaning that all operations that were invoked through the Composer REST server that is listening on port `3003` are related to the `Consumer` with identifier 5. For example, if a new `Consumer` participant is created (let's say ID 6), then a new business card must be issued to the participant, and another instance of a Composer REST server must be started using the new card.

In most use cases, a single business card is enough for an entire organization. Other rules for issuing business cards can be defined by governance, such as a business card per branch/subsidiary, or each user must have their own business card.

At this point, you should have five instances of the Composer REST server running on your computer, and each one should be capable of being accessed through a browser at the following address: `http://localhost:<port>`.

Creating the IoT part of the solution

After defining the entire blockchain network and getting everything up and running, we will now set up and develop the device that's going to update the ledger with box and pallet measurements.

To complete that, we're going to create a new device, using the same approach as `Chapter 2`, *Creating Your First IoT Solution*, and create an application that receives events from measurements and updates the blockchain ledger using the API that was exposed by the Composer REST server.

Hardware setup

To assemble this monitoring device, we will apply a couple of assumptions that might be pertinent to a production environment:

- The transporting vehicle has a Wi-Fi connection available so that the device can connect to the internet
- The monitoring device time is synchronized with the application time, including the time zone
- All boxes are transported at the same time, using the same vehicle, so that the same conditions and measurements apply to all boxes in a pallet

In a production-level application, these restrictions/assumptions have to be handled with techniques such as caching non-published events and using different network providers (Sigfox, LoRAWan, mobile connections, and so on), and the actual time must be synchronized with the device's location.

The parts that are used in this project are shown here:

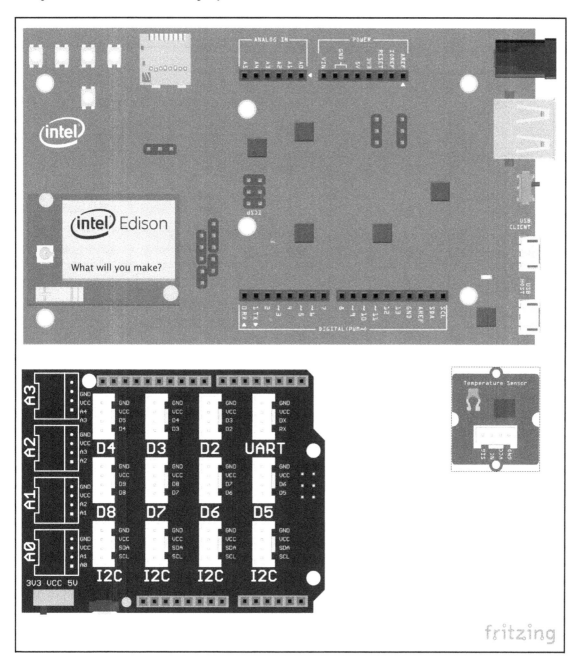

This image was created with Fritzing and is licensed under CC BY-SA 3.0; see https://creativecommons.org/licenses/by-sa/3.0/

The description of each component is given in the following table. You should be familiar with them, given that they are a subset of what was used in Chapter 2, *Creating Your First IoT Solution*:

Quantity	Component
1	Intel Edison module
1	Intel Edison Arduino breakout board
1	Grove Base Shield v2
1	Grove Temperature Sensor v1.2
1	Grove universal 4-pin cable

Given these assumptions, the device that's used in this application is connected, as shown in the following diagram. Here, we have attached the Grove Temperature Sensor to the A3 connection jack in the Base Shield:

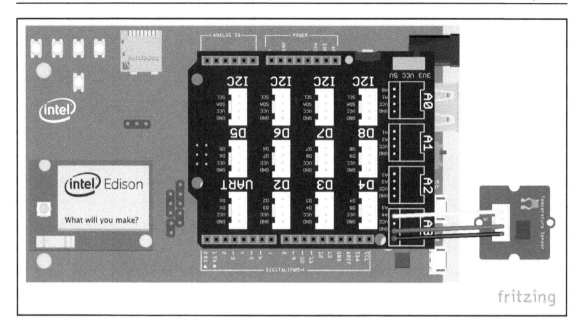

This completes the device that will monitor food box transportation.

Firmware development

The following code has been borrowed from `Chapter 2`, *Creating Your First IoT Solution*, since it has the same hardware characteristics and the same objectives.

The only modification is in the published JSON: we have to remove the `soilMoisture` property and add the box ID when transporting from the factory to the warehouse, and add the pallet ID when transporting from the warehouse to the store.

It retrieves the temperature of the Grove sensor and publishes it to the Watson IoT platform:

```
var iotf = require("ibmiotf");
var mraa = require('mraa');
var config = require("./device.json");
var deviceClient = new iotf.IotfDevice(config);
var temperatureSensor = new mraa.Aio(3);

var RESISTOR = 100000;
var THERMISTOR = 4250;
```

```
var getTemperature = function() {
    var sensorReading = temperatureSensor.read();
    var R = 1023 / sensorReading - 1;
    R = RESISTOR * R;
    var temperature = 1 /
(Math.log(R/RESISTOR)/THERMISTOR+1/298.15)-273.15;
    return temperature;
};

deviceClient.connect();
deviceClient.on('connect', function(){
    console.log("connected");
    setInterval(function function_name () {
// When transporting from Factory to Warehouse
    deviceClient.publish('status','json','{ "foodBoxId":"1",
"temperature":+          getTemperature()}',          2);

// When transporting from Warehouse to Store
// deviceClient.publish('status','json','{ "palletId":"1", "temperature":+
// getTemperature()}', 2);

  },300000);
});
```

Application development

Since we are running the Hyperledger environment locally, the application being developed here has to run on the same network as Hyperledger. Given that we're not running it in IBM Cloud/Bluemix, the configuration will be stored in a JSON file, in the same directory that the main .js file of the application will run in.

The content structure of the configuration JSON file is listed here and must be updated with the details that were defined in Chapter 2, *Creating Your First IoT Solution*:

```
{
    "org": "<your IoT organization id>",
    "id": "sample-app",
    "auth-key": "<application authentication key>",
    "auth-token": "<application authentication token>"
}
```

The application code receives all of the events that were published by the device and updates the `FoodBoxes` in the pallet with the temperature gathered:

```
// Composer Rest Server definitions
var request = require('request');
var UPDATE_BOX_URL = "http://<composer rest server
url>:3004/api/UpdateFoodBoxTransportationData"
var UPDATE_PALLET_URL = "http://<composer rest server
url>:3004/api/UpdateTransportationData"

// Watson IoT definitions
var Client = require("ibmiotf");
var appClientConfig = require("./application.json");
var appClient = new Client.IotfApplication(appClientConfig);

appClient.connect();]

appClient.on("connect", function () {
 appClient.subscribeToDeviceEvents();
});

appClient.on("deviceEvent", function (deviceType, deviceId, eventType,
format, payload) {
 // update food box
 // updateFoodBox(payload.temperature);
 // update pallet
 // updatePallet(payload.temperature);
 });
```

The following code calls the defined transaction in the blockchain network through the Composer REST server:

```
var updateFoodBox = function (temperature) {
    var options = {
        uri: UPDATE_BOX_URL,
        method: 'POST',
        json: {
    "$class":
"com.packtpublishing.businessnetwork.foodsafety.UpdateFoodBoxTransportation
Data",
    "asset":
"resource:com.packtpublishing.businessnetwork.foodsafety.FoodBox#<YOUR
FOODBOX ID>",
    "locationInformation": {
      "$class": "com.packtpublishing.businessnetwork.foodsafety.Location",
      "date": "2018-12-24T15:08:27.912Z",
      "location": "<LOCATION TYPE>",
      "locationIdentifier": "<LOCATION ID>",
```

```
        "status": "<LOCATION STATUS>"
      },
      "measurementInformation": {
        "$class": "com.packtpublishing.businessnetwork.foodsafety.Measurement",
        "date": "2018-12-24T15:08:27.912Z",
        "value": 0
      }
    }
        };
    }


var updatePallet = function (temperature) {
    var options = {
       uri: UPDATE_BOX_URL,
       method: 'POST',
       json: {
      "$class":
"com.packtpublishing.businessnetwork.foodsafety.UpdateTransportationData",
      "asset":
"resource:com.packtpublishing.businessnetwork.foodsafety.FoodBoxPallet#<YOU
R PALLET ID>",
      "locationInformation": {
        "$class": "com.packtpublishing.businessnetwork.foodsafety.Location",
        "date": "2018-12-24T15:09:02.944Z",
        "location": "<LOCATION TYPE>",
        "locationIdentifier": "<LOCATION ID>",
        "status": "<STATUS>"
      },
      "measurementInformation": {
        "$class": "com.packtpublishing.businessnetwork.foodsafety.Measurement",
        "date": "2018-12-24T15:09:02.944Z",
        "value": 0
      }
    }
        };
    }
```

End-to-end testing

For testing purposes, we are going to use the Hyperledger Composer Playground for most of the operations, except transporter updates. So, at this point, you can stop all of the Composer REST servers that were started in the previous section, except the one that was started for the transporter participant (listening on port 3004).

If your Hyperledger Composer Playground was installed during the development environment setup, all you have to do is run the `composer-playground` command, or install it using npm (`npm install -g composer-playground`).

Your default browser will open the **Composer-Playground** web application, as shown in the following screenshot:

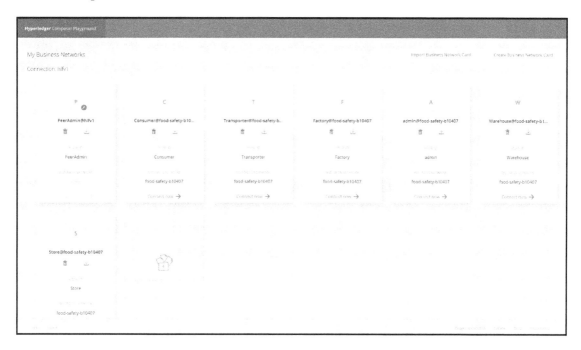

Composer playground landing page

You can see the same participants that were created earlier.

Creating a FoodBox

As per the permissions we've granted, factories can create `FoodBoxes`. Let's see how:

1. Find the **Factory 1 @food-safety-b10407** business card and select the **Connect now** option. Then, click on **Test** at the top left of the screen.

2. In the left-hand panel, select **Assets -> FoodBox,** and in the upper-right corner, click on **+ Create New Asset:**

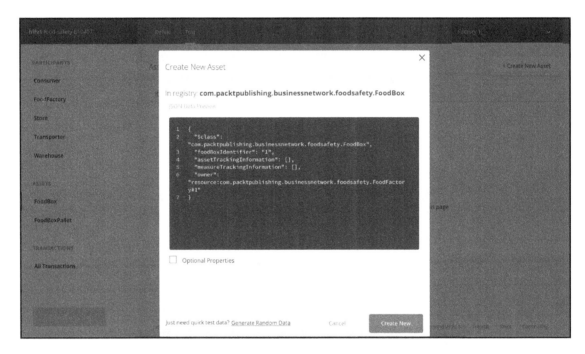

3. Fill up the JSON with the following content and create the asset using the **Create New** button:

```
{
  "$class":
"com.packtpublishing.businessnetwork.foodsafety.FoodBox",
  "foodBoxIdentifier": "2015",
  "assetTrackingInformation": [],
  "measureTrackingInformation": [],
  "owner":
"resource:com.packtpublishing.businessnetwork.foodsafety.FoodFactor
y#1"
}
```

Transferring the asset to the transporter

To transfer an asset of the food safety network using the Hyperledger Composer Playground, take the following steps:

1. In the top-right corner of the application, select the **My business networks** option and connect as transporter.

2. If you select **Test**, **Assets** → **FoodBox**, you will see that there are no assets available:

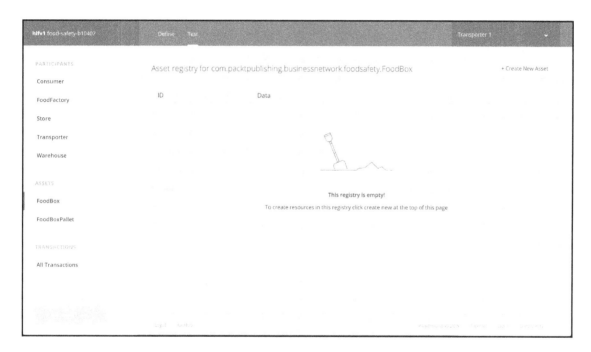

3. Return to the `Factory` identity, select the **Edit** button on the right-hand side of the asset data, and update the JSON file with the following data:

```
{
  "$class":
"com.packtpublishing.businessnetwork.foodsafety.FoodBox",
  "foodBoxIdentifier": "1",
  "assetTrackingInformation": [],
  "measureTrackingInformation": [],
  "owner":
"resource:com.packtpublishing.businessnetwork.foodsafety.Transporte
r#2"
}
```

4. Save the asset; it will disappear from the Factory view. When you return to the Transporter view, you will find that the transporter can now see the asset.

Measuring the temperature while transporting

At this point, we will simulate temperature measurements during transportation.

We created the following commented code in the IoT application code because we are handling transportation gathering data at two different points in time.

The first is when a `FoodBox` is transported from the `Factory` to the `Warehouse`, which is implemented by the `updateFoodBox` function, while the `updatePallet` function is aimed at processing the transportation from the `Warehouse` to the store:

```
appClient.on("deviceEvent", function (deviceType, deviceId, eventType,
format, payload) {
 // update food box
 // updateFoodBox(payload.temperature);
 // update pallet
 // updatePallet(payload.temperature);
 });
```

At this point, we are handling the transportation from the `Factory` to the `Warehouse`, so uncomment line 19 of the code—`updateFoodBox(payload.temperature);`—and then update lines 30, 34, 35, and 36, providing the correct values for the data.

Ensure that the Composer REST server for the transporter is up and running and that the URLs defined in lines 2 and 3 of the device code are pointing to the correct Composer REST server host.

Start the device application.

Transferring the asset to the warehouse

The same thing happens when the asset is transferred to the transporter. Go to the asset view of the transporter, edit the JSON file, and change the owner with the respective value:

```
"owner":
"resource:com.packtpublishing.businessnetwork.foodsafety.Warehouse#3"
```

Creating a pallet and adding the box to it

To create a pallet, we need to follow the same process as that for a FoodBox:

1. In the left-hand panel, select **Assets → FoodBoxPallet**, and in the upper-right corner, click on **+ Create New Asset**.

2. Then, fill the JSON with the following data. Make sure that you were using the same FoodBox ID in the `foodBoxInPallet` field and the Warehouse ID (3) in the `owner` field:

```
{
  "$class": "org.hyperledger.composer.system.AddAsset",
  "resources": [
  {
  "$class":
"com.packtpublishing.businessnetwork.foodsafety.FoodBoxPallet",
  "foodBoxPalletIdentifier": "3485",
  "foodBoxInPallet":
"resource:com.packtpublishing.businessnetwork.foodsafety.FoodBox#24
73",
  "assetTrackingInformation": [],
  "measureTrackingInformation": [],
  "owner":
"resource:com.packtpublishing.businessnetwork.foodsafety.Warehouse#
3"
  }
  ],
  "targetRegistry":
"resource:org.hyperledger.composer.system.AssetRegistry#com.packtpu
blishing.businessnetwork.foodsafety.FoodBoxPallet",
  "transactionId":
"0dfe3b672a78dd1d6728acd763d125f813ed0ca74450a2596b9cf79f47f054ad",
  "timestamp": "2018-12-24T14:43:34.217Z"
}
```

3. After creating the pallet, transfer both the pallet and box to the transporter, as before. The owner value of the JSON should be as follows:

```
  "owner":
"resource:com.packtpublishing.businessnetwork.foodsafety.Transporte
r#2"
```

Measuring the temperature while transporting a pallet

This follows the same rules as the measurements for the FoodBox transportation, but you have to comment line 19 and uncomment line 20 of the device code, as well as update lines 53, 57, 58, and 59 with the correct values for your pallet.

At the end of the transportation, transfer the asset to the store by using the `owner` of the pallet and the box with the following line:

```
"owner": "resource:com.packtpublishing.businessnetwork.foodsafety.Store#4"
```

Tracking the FoodBox

To track the food box as a consumer, we're going to use the Hyperledger Composer Historian through `composer-playground`.

To access the history of actions that have been applied to an asset, connect to the Hyperledger environment using the Consumer business card and select the **All Transactions** option from the left-hand panel of the playground.

We will be able to see all of the transactions that have been performed on an asset, from its creation to the arrival of the pallet and its inner boxes to the store:

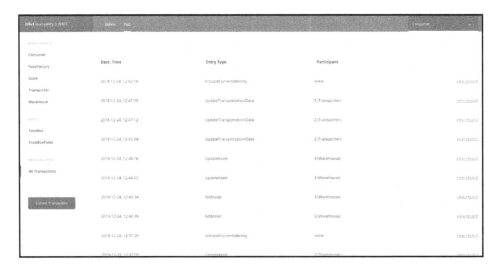

Composer playground - Historian

We can also see the transaction details by clicking on the **view record** link, as shown here:

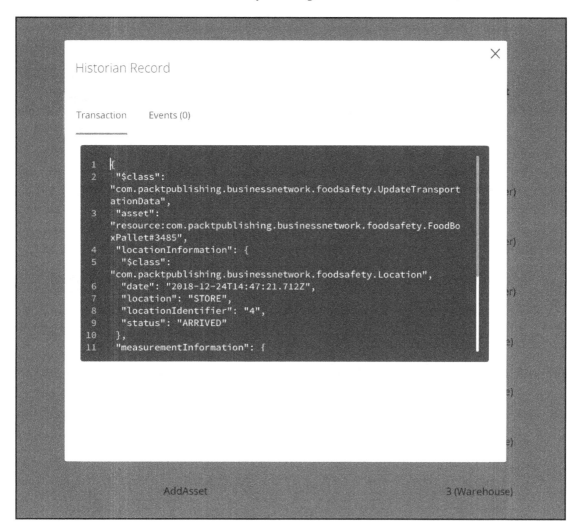

Summary

In this chapter, we learned how to create a business network using Hyperledger Composer and the Watson IoT Platform.

In the process of developing the solution, we were able to create a Hyperledger Composer project using Yeoman; define shared data structures; create assets, participants transactions, and access control lists; as well as create the first version of a network and upgrade it to a newer version.

We were also able to create a device that is responsible for reading temperatures from the hypothetical transport of a food box from a factory to a warehouse, and later, from the warehouse to a store, and added that information to the food box asset in the shared ledger of the blockchain network.

The consumer of that food box was also able to track the information related to that box from the very beginning of the production chain.

Even though Hyperledger Composer and Watson IoT development are quite simple, the solution that we've created addresses a huge problem regarding safety in the food chain.

The following chapters will give you the author's point of view about lessons learned, practices, and patterns used in real-world projects, and how IoT and blockchain are necessary tools for creating business models and addressing new challenges in the current Industry 4.0 scenario.

8
The IoT, Blockchain, and Industry 4.0

The IoT and blockchain are not the only sets of technologies that are driving the evolution of a new economic and manufacturing revolution. **Industry 4.0** is a concept that takes place in an era of new methods, technologies, and unprecedented computing capabilities that can be used by anyone who has internet access.

In this chapter, we will explore the role of key technologies such as the IoT, blockchain, and cloud computing, focusing on how these factors are driving the evolution of Industry 4.0.

The following topics will be covered in this chapter:

- The role of cloud computing in the new economy model
- How the IoT can help innovate industries
- Blockchain as a business platform for Industry 4.0

Industry 4.0

Industry 4.0, also known as **Economy 4.0**, is the name given to a new manufacturing model where connectivity and data collection and processing are widely applied throughout an entire manufacturing chain.

Smart factories differentiate themselves from automated factories because they are not simply automated; they are connected, monitorable, and cooperative.

It's important to know that Industry 4.0 is not only related to manufacturing; it can be understood as the creation of new manufacturing models designed to create more personalized and engaging experiences. The new model emphasizes that having data is a key factor for success, and new business models are being created at the intersection of current business models. Cloud computing, the IoT, cognitive computing, and blockchain are some of the technologies that have been driving this new model.

Cloud computing as an innovation platform

Cloud computing is providing opportunities to create new business models, as well as providing tooling to redesign existing ones. Cloud computing creates simple, self-service, flexible, and low-cost infrastructure for a highly technological and innovative ecosystem of services. More than processing capability, the role of cloud computing is to become an innovation platform. Let's dive into the world of cloud computing to understand its relation and importance to Industry 4.0 development.

The cloud computing model

Cloud computing is the concept of sharing computational resources, including memory, calculation, networking, and storage capabilities, to run applications. The characteristics that define a computing model as a cloud model include self-service resource allocation, software-defined resources, and pay-as-you-go monetization. These are usually presented in three models of commercialization: **Infrastructure as a Service (IaaS)**, **Platform as a Service (PaaS)**, and **Software as a Service (SaaS)**. Furthermore, they can be delivered into public and private models of deployment:

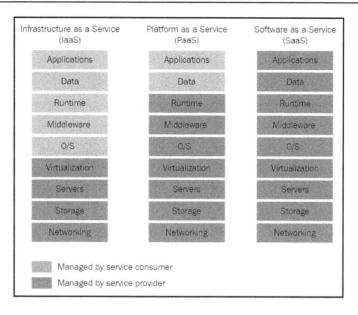

Looking at the delivery models in the preceding diagram, it's possible to understand which capabilities the service consumer should care about:

- In the **IaaS** model, as the name says, the cloud service provider is responsible for maintaining networking, storage, servers, and virtual machine components. Every layer above that, including its licenses, backups, updates, and upgrades, are the responsibility of the party that contracted the service.
- **PaaS** provides three more layers: operating system, middleware, and runtime capabilities, giving the service consumer more abstraction on infrastructure and software license management; the only layers they have to deal with are the application code and binaries and data used by it.
- **SaaS** takes computing to a higher level of abstraction: all the service consumer has to do is to use the subscribed solution.

IBM Cloud Public (also known as Bluemix) provides all of the capabilities described here. IaaS, PaaS, and SaaS solutions are available through its console. You can instantiate physical or virtual machines and application runtimes, and subscribe to any of the services available through the service catalog, including the IBM Watson IoT and IBM Blockchain platforms.

When these models are deployed in a multi-tenant environment in a public network such as the internet, it's called a public cloud—a place where a person and a company share the same resources. When a company or a person uses any of these models in a single-tenant environment in a private or public network, it is called a private cloud.

The importance of cloud computing to Industry 4.0

Before the cloud computing model, IT departments had a long, expensive, and hard path to follow to make a solution available to its customers. They had to buy servers; wait for delivery; provision space in their data centers; prepare networking and virtualization; install operation systems, middleware, databases, and runtimes; and then develop applications and deploy them to the production environment.

When cloud computing takes place in the same scenario as presented above, provisioning the same computing capabilities and start developing applications happens in a matter of minutes. You will only need to pay for the use of the resource.

When developing innovative solutions minimum viable products (MVPs) may not have expected results leading to constant changes in infrastructure, platform software and attached services. What if the MVP created does not fit target users need? In the first scenario, you already paid for all the resources you needed, so even if you shut down the solution, you already spent capex. However, in the second scenario (cloud), you paid for the service, so it's just opex. What if the solution had a great fit and people are using it a lot? In the first scenario, you have to follow an easier (but still hard) path to provision more resources, while in cloud computing, you can scale the solution resources whenever they are needed, not all the time.

Cloud computing also provides the ability to test new services and create new applications using best-of-breed services and technologies such as the IoT, cognitive computing, blockchain, and other services that are created and delivered on the internet. Those services are powerful tools to create new solutions and business models, providing a differentiated experience to clients whether there are 1, 10, 100, or 1 million people using the same service.

The IoT

As previously described, data is a key factor in the success of Industry 4.0. The more data collected and analyzed, the more assertive predictions and recommendations become.

More than an automation framework technology, the IoT is a great way to collect a huge amount of data from connected devices. By combining different data sources (machine and robot sensors, security cameras, heart-rate monitors, environment and meteorological data), it is possible to define and analyze domains to understand the current reality of business contexts and have a more reasoned analysis of it. It is also possible to have insights on how to become more productive, more predictable, and more flexible, because you can process the data as it is collected in real time, as shown in the following diagram:

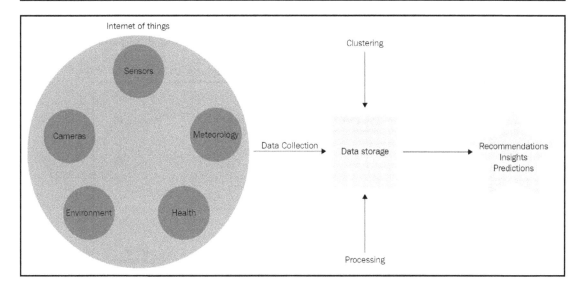

The results of the processing can also become a trigger to change the actions machines and robots are running at the moment, even to fix a defect in the product that is being created to perform self-healing tasks before continuing a process.

Blockchain – simplifying business chains

As business models evolve, they tend to have a leaner approach. In this context, a lean industry is meant to focus only on things that have value to the target client of the product. Whatever procedure, part of the product, or process that creates it that does not provide value to the product is considered useless and must be removed or changed so it adds more value to the end-to-end solution. With the same approach, smart business models tend to only have steps that add value and knowledge to the business model, which means that outsourcing is still a big deal in this area. Becoming lean is not easy and cheap if you don't know how to integrate the end-to-end service chain into the business.

Blockchain comes into action when outsourcing or decentralizing business tasks are vital to the model, by giving the opportunity to decentralize tasks. Let's take a look at a traditional car sales process in the following diagram:

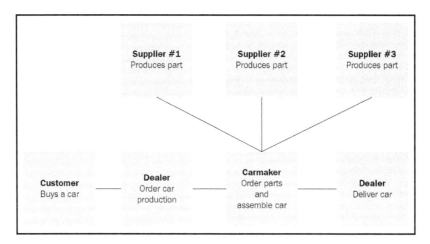

Whenever a customer buys a car, a new entry for that car is created in the dealer's ledger and an order is placed to the carmaker, which creates another entry into its ledger and orders parts from its suppliers, and this also creates order entries in their ledgers. Blockchain simplifies the process by using a shared ledger for all stakeholders of the process:

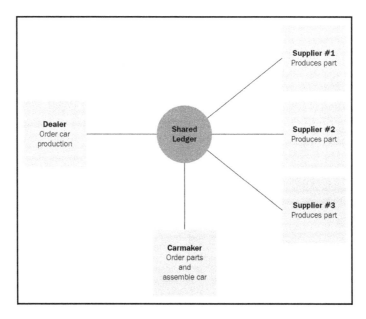

The process itself is now auditable by design and the final product can be tracked end to end, giving the new car's owner knowledge about the origin of the product.

Blockchain enables a product-driven business process that is both lean and auditable.

Summary

In this chapter, you gained an understanding of the importance of key technologies such as cloud computing, the IoT, and blockchain in the context of Industry 4.0.

Cloud computing is a computing model that provides low-cost, scalable, and self-service technology adoption, creating an environment that is suitable for creating innovative business models.

The IoT is more than an automation toolkit, and can be placed as a framework for data collection and creating a digital context that is similar to the real-world context; it creates a digitized reality context, simulating the same conditions as the real world.

Blockchain enables lean production lines by simplifying the process of decentralization and helps companies to focus on their strengths, without spending time and money on tasks that do not generate aggregated value for the final product.

In the next chapter, we will look at best practices and lessons learned from previous projects that address some problems we faced and how those issues were addressed.

9
Best Practices for Developing Blockchain and IoT Solutions

As is the case for every emerging technology, being an early adopter is full of challenges and lessons that need to be learned. The focus of this chapter is to present some solutions that we can apply to real-world projects in order to avoid getting into trouble.

The following topics will be covered in this chapter:

- Reference architecture for cloud applications
- How to create cloud-native applications using the 12-factor application development model
- Serverless computing
- Using Hyperledger Composer as an accelerator for application development

Developing cloud applications

There are many potential pitfalls related to cloud applications, ranging from the simple misuse of resources to unsolvable problems. Applying a concise architecture and using the 12-factor application development pattern ensures you won't get into trouble when the application scales up or down.

A container is a standardized way to package an application with all its dependencies, including its code, runtimes, middleware, libraries, and operating system. Docker and Garden are containers that can be run in the IBM Cloud Platform, but there are other container types that can also be used, such as Rockt. Using containers increases the portability of an application, so it doesn't matter if the host operating system is one particular distribution of Linux and your application was built on a different distribution, because the operating system is a layer of the containerized application and both distributions are shipped together.

The following diagram demonstrates the structure of a containerized application:

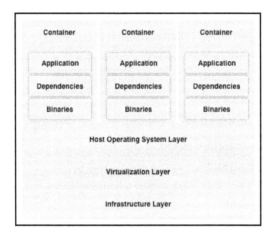

Cloud platforms use containerized applications and deploy them into a set of servers. We can move these applications inside the flexible computing environment to make better use of the existing infrastructure and to keep track of the containers deployed in the service discovery component.

Each platform has its own way of using the containerized model of application deployment, as shown in the following diagram:

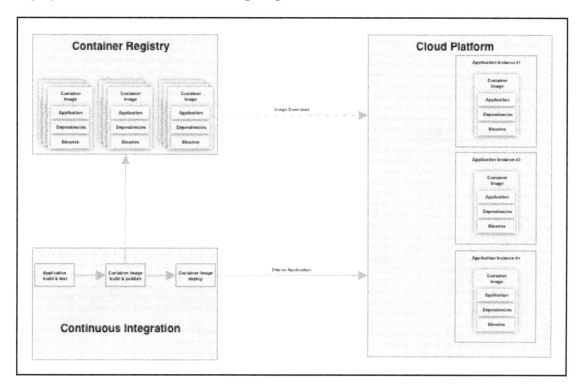

A container is deployed based on a container image, which is a read-only definition of the base image, the dependencies, and the application. Each container of the same application is deployed based on that image, and any changes made to the container during runtime exist only while that container is active, and only apply to to that instance of the container.

Reference architecture

Cloud computing creates an abstract environment for deploying applications; we use virtual runtimes. This means that we have no location awareness and no assurance that our application will stay in the same data center or virtual machine. We cannot even trust that the IP address of the application will remain the same after 10 minutes. The following diagram shows a successfully applied reference architecture for cloud applications using IBM Cloud Public (Bluemix):

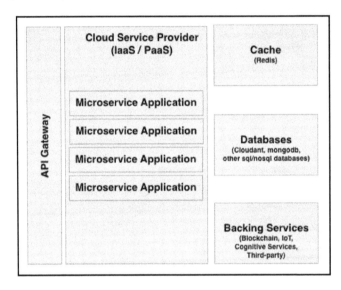

Cloud-native applications should scale horizontally, which means that whenever the workload demand increases, the application should increase the number of instances of that application to handle new requests. Similarly, if the workload decreases, the number of application instances should be decreased.

Development using the 12–factor application model

The 12-factor application model is a set of practices that should be followed in order to make cloud applications scalable. It provides support for hostile cloud environment changes.

The 12 principles of the model are as follows:

- **Code base:** Our codebase is tracked in revision control and is deployed many times
- **Dependencies:** We should explicitly declare and isolate dependencies
- **Configuration:** We should store the application configuration parameters in the environment
- **Backing services:** We should treat backing services as attached resources
- **Build, release, run:** We should strictly separate build and run stages
- **Processes:** We should execute the app as one or more stateless processes
- **Port binding:** We should export services via port binding
- **Concurrency:** We should scale out via the process model
- **Disposability:** We should maximize robustness with fast startup and graceful shutdown
- **Development/production parity:** We should keep development, staging, and production as similar as possible
- **Logs:** We should treat logs as event streams
- **Admin processes:** We should run administration and management tasks as one-off processes

These principles decrease the number of simple errors related to cloud computing.

You don't have to apply all these concepts to all cloud-native applications that you develop. For example, if you don't need a script to preload a database, you do not need to apply the admin processes principle. However, if you are using an application that needs to keep a state or share the state with different applications (such as sessions), using backing services is essential because you never know what physical or virtual computer host the container that responds to the user requests is located.

Serverless computing

Serverless computing is a model of deployment in which an application is deployed in an environment but is not necessarily running all the time. Its container is started when it is first executed and is kept alive while requests demand its execution. After a period of inactivity, the container for that application is quiesced. It is important to note that stopped containers will take time to get started, so real-time responsiveness is not a strength of a serverless application.

A serverless application (or, as many cloud service providers call it, a cloud function) is a microservice that is deployed and attached to a trigger, which is responsible for starting the container with the function and running it. A trigger might be a database change, a message delivered to a broker, an HTTP request, or another type of request.

Cloud providers usually charge the execution of cloud functions based on the duration of their execution and their resource allocation (usually memory). For example, a cloud function might take 500 milliseconds and use 256 MB of memory.

A successful cloud function is not computing-intensive and does not have a large number of requests (scheduled procedures). To facilitate the process of building and deploying serverless applications, the serverless framework is a good choice since it supports Google Cloud, AWS, IBM Cloud, and Microsoft Azure implementations of serverless computing.

Blockchain development using Hyperledger Composer

Hyperledger Composer is a project hosted by the Linux Foundation under the Hyperledger brand. The project aims to create a framework and toolset to accelerate the development of blockchain applications using Hyperledger Fabric, and simplify integration with other applications. It is important to bear in mind that any framework intends to simplify an aspect of a solution by abstracting some of its complexity, but that it also restricts control over the abstraction applied.

The Hyperledger Composer toolkit

Hyperledger Composer is not a universal solution to all the complexities presented by Hyperledger Fabric. It takes away some of the flexibility over tasks that could be customized without it. What it does do, however, is supply a toolkit to create chaincode projects, build blockchain application packages (`.bna` files), and deploy them to Hyperledger Fabric.

The development of a business network using Hyperledger Composer is focused on creating assets, participants, transactions, queries, and access control lists using a project structure and a common language. After creating the business network definition, Composer has tools to package and deploy the application to a Hyperledger Fabric platform.

The Hyperledger Composer REST server

To simplify integration with other applications, Hyperledger Composer provides the Composer REST server, an API server built on top of a LoopBack framework that connects to the business network defined. It retrieves information on assets, transactions, and participants, and provides a REST API server and and the service contract described in swagger format to interact with the business network out of the box.

The Composer REST server ships with many useful features. The ones that are most worth taking a look at are authentication, multiuser mode, and data source configuration.

Authentication and multiuser mode

It's not unusual to request authentication when you are creating business applications. The Composer REST server provides the means to connect to many authentication and authorization providers, using Passport middleware. While the project claims that Passport has over 300 strategies for authentication and authorization, our experience has shown that not all of these work out of the box; sometimes, you have to create custom code in order to make them work. We have, however, successfully implemented Google, GitHub, Auth0, and LDAP authentication strategies out of the box.

Multiuser mode allows the use of a single Composer REST server for multiple participants, instead of deploying a distinct Composer REST server for each participant. In this mode, the API is retrieved using a master business card, but the interaction with the business network is done using its own business card. This mode requires user authentication to be enabled.

Data source configuration

The Composer REST server uses data sources to store user session data. This doesn't mean that it has to have an explicit data source configured; if no data source is configured, the Composer REST server uses an out-of-the box memory connector.

When using multiple instances of the Composer REST server for high availability or load balancing, the instances do not share memory, so a data source is required. Any data source that has a loopback connector available can be used. In our experience, MongoDB, Cloudant, and Redis work out of the box; we just need to install the connector and configure the environment variables by following the steps provided by the Hyperledger.

Summary

In this chapter, we have looked at the implications of developing and deploying applications to a cloud environment. We have considered how containers work, how to deploy containerized applications to a cloud platform, and an alternative model: serverless computing. We also presented the 12-factor model principles for the development of cloud-native applications.

We then looked at Hyperledger Composer as an accelerator for developing blockchain solutions. We explored various features, including using authentication, multiuser mode, and data source configuration.

This book provides information on creating simple applications using IBM Watson IoT Platform and Hyperledger Compose. These are far from being the only platforms and tools that support IoT and blockchain solutions, but the concepts are the same and can be applied. If you are interested in extending capabilities with the explained tools, both Watson IoT and Hyperledger Fabric / Composer, provide extensive documentation on how to use them as well as a large number of community provided articles through out the internet but, our thought is that practice is the best way to understand whether they fit or not to a given solution so, even if you do want to learn how to use the toolkit, just try, simple use cases are good teachers.

Further reading

The topics presented by this chapter are an overview and if you need more depth on any topics we recommend reading the following references:

- The 12-factor application methodology : `https://12factor.net/`
- The serverless framework: `https://serverless.com/`
- Hyperledger Composer: `https://hyperledger.github.io/composer`

Other Books You May Enjoy

If you enjoyed this book, you may be interested in these other books by Packt:

Hands-On Cybersecurity with Blockchain
Rajneesh Gupta

ISBN: 9781788990189

- Understand the cyberthreat landscape
- Learn about Ethereum and Hyperledger Blockchain
- Program Blockchain solutions
- Build Blockchain-based apps for 2FA, and DDoS protection
- Develop Blockchain-based PKI solutions and apps for storing DNS entries
- Challenges and the future of cybersecurity and Blockchain

Practical Internet of Things with JavaScript
Arvind Ravulavaru

ISBN: 9781788292948

- Integrate sensors and actuators with the cloud and control them for your Smart Weather Station.
- Develop your very own Amazon Alexa integrating with your IoT solution
- Define custom rules and execute jobs on certain data events using IFTTT
- Build a simple surveillance solutions using Amazon Recognition & Raspberry Pi 3
- Design a fall detection system and build a notification system for it.
- Use Amazon Rekognition for face detection and face recognition in your Surveillance project

Leave a review - let other readers know what you think

Please share your thoughts on this book with others by leaving a review on the site that you bought it from. If you purchased the book from Amazon, please leave us an honest review on this book's Amazon page. This is vital so that other potential readers can see and use your unbiased opinion to make purchasing decisions, we can understand what our customers think about our products, and our authors can see your feedback on the title that they have worked with Packt to create. It will only take a few minutes of your time, but is valuable to other potential customers, our authors, and Packt. Thank you!

Index